Praise for *Only as The Day Is Long*

"Dorianne Laux has written about love and violence, survival and grief, in poems that are clear, compelling and insightful. . . . [Laux] shows us how to endure hardships without losing humanity and compassion. This timely, beautifully crafted collection wonderfully balances light and dark." —Elizabeth Lund, *Washington Post*

"[I've] been savoring Dorianne Laux's *Only as the Day Is Long: New and Selected Poems*. . . . [I]was blown away by the newer poems about her mother in particular. You may want this book on your bedside table this summer, too. I know it will stay on mine—with a pen close by." —Maggie Smith, *Kenyon Review*

"Laux's work has always felt subversive in its unapologetic celebration of female sexuality, but now she proves herself one of our most daring contemporary poets with *Only as the Day Is Long: New and Selected Poems*. . . . From formal sonnets to narrative sequences, Laux's rhythmic lines merge song with story and illuminate the nature of grief and loss. . . . Laux anchors her poems in sensory details, transforming simple acts into lyric moments. . . . We're lucky. *Only as the Day Is Long* gives us Laux's lyric powers evolving over the course of her career, resonant with courage and compassion." —Diana Whitney, *San Francisco Chronicle*

"Laux writes with startling directness of the physical and sexual abuse she and her sister suffered at the hands of her father. . . . But there are other poems, just as frank and openhearted, that celebrate the wondrousness of sex (so skillfully that fiction writers should take note). . . . Beyond her admirable tenacity and spirit, Laux is just plain wise—and refreshingly unpretentious in her wisdom. . . . Laux's new poems arrive at the end of the collection as a perfect finale." —Jonathan Russell Clark, *Vulture*

T0025557

"Unflinching. . . . Helpless but not hapless, [Laux] deftly writes of heartbreak—the absolute, gutting, severe loss of the one who brought her into this world. . . . Laux is majestic. . . . The elegies accumulate, settle into our throats, drill down—her selected poems are gorgeous to revisit, but these new pieces are symphonic—and they become a perfect coda of grief."   —Nick Ripatrazone, *Millions*

"The ability to write accessible poetry is proof that Laux is an expert. She captures human sentiment and weaves emotions into multisensory landscapes with accurate details. Rich with detailed, layered poems, *Only As the Day Is Long: New and Selected Poems* is a collection of Laux's finest. . . . A necessary addition to a home library."
                              —Andrew Jarvis, *New York Journal of Books*

"When Laux welcomes readers into a personal moment, she speaks for humankind. . . . This is a catalogue of honest work, from beginning to end."   —*Publishers Weekly*, starred review

"Dorianne Laux is one of those poets I turn to again and again for cradling beauty and darkness so close together in a poem."
                              —Aimee Nezhukumatathil, author of *Oceanic*

"Another splendid new one by one of our best, who never stops paying attention, and is never unwilling, and summons from her readers unwavering trust."   —Mark Doty, author of *Deep Lane*

"Throughout the years and throughout her five books Dorianne Laux has not faltered. She has wrestled with the angels and with the serpents; Eros and Thanatos are wrestling still, and the sound they make is the sound of this woman singing."
                              —Marie Howe, author of *Magdalene*

"Dorianne Laux's *Only as the Day Is Long: New and Selected Poems* gifts the reader with a foundation that bears the true weight of life and death. Each trope rises out of lived feeling—everyday rituals bend toward the sacred as beauty peers through a pure, honest language. Here, at the heart of mastery, is an American voice paying dues through tribute. These poems dare to sing and cross borders, in step with the natural and universal."

—Yusef Komunyakaa, author of *The Emperor of Water Clocks*

"In a vast ocean of too-much-to-read out there, I can always find an island of sanity in Laux's work, and within individual poems, always, always spots of light and breath and truth."

—Lia Purpura, author of *It Shouldn't Have Been Beautiful*

"A prodigious imagination that somehow manages to sift through the ordinary, quotidian, and squalid realities of our world, to produce moments of grace and shimmering beauty, and empathetic illumination. Dorianne Laux is a national treasure, a poet of immense insight and masterful craft. . . . *Only as the Day Is Long* is a tour de force, a work of striking beauty and humanity—a work for its own time."

—Kwame Dawes, author of *City of Bones: A Testament*

ALSO BY DORIANNE LAUX

The Book of Men

Facts About the Moon

Smoke

What We Carry

Awake

The Poet's Companion:
A Guide to the Pleasures of Writing Poetry
(with Kim Addonizio)

The Mothers

Salt

Duet

The Book of Women

ONLY AS THE DAY IS LONG

NEW AND SELECTED POEMS

DORIANNE LAUX

W. W. NORTON & COMPANY
Independent Publishers Since 1923

FOR MY SISTER,

Mary-Ellen (1955–2017)

Dorianne Laux, "Death Comes to Me Again, a Girl," "Fear," "Last Words,"
"Trying to Raise the Dead," "The Shopfitter's Wife," "Abschied Symphony," "The Line,"
"Family Stories," "Pearl," and "Smoke" from *Smoke*. Copyright © 2000 by Dorianne Laux.
Reprinted with the permission of BOA Editions, Ltd., www.boaeditions.org.

Dorianne Laux, "After Twelve Days of Rain," "Aphasia," "What We Carry," "Dust,"
"Twelve," Fast Gas," "As It Is," "The Thief," "This Close," "The Loves," and "Kissing"
from *What We Carry*. Copyright © 1994 by Dorianne Laux. Reprinted with the
permission of BOA Editions, Ltd., www.boaeditions.org.

For information about permission to reproduce selections from this book, write to
Permissions, W. W. Norton & Company, Inc., 500 Fifth Avenue, New York, NY 10110

For information about special discounts for bulk purchases, please contact
W. W. Norton Special Sales at specialsales@wwnorton.com or 800-233-4830

Manufacturing by LSC Harrisonburg
Book design by JAM Design
Production manager: Lauren Abbate

Library of Congress Cataloging-in-Publication Data

Names: Laux, Dorianne, author.
Title: Only as the day is long : new and selected poems / Dorianne Laux.
Description: First edition. | New York : W. W. Norton & Company, [2019] | Includes index.
Identifiers: LCCN 2018038026 | ISBN 9780393652338 (hardcover)
Classification: LCC PS3562.A8455 A6 2019 | DDC 811/.54—dc23
LC record available at https://lccn.loc.gov/2018038026

ISBN 978-0-393-35819-3 pbk.

W. W. Norton & Company, Inc., 500 Fifth Avenue, New York, N.Y. 10110
www.wwnorton.com

W. W. Norton & Company Ltd., 15 Carlisle Street, London W1D 3BS

3 4 5 6 7 8 9 0

Contents

from SMOKE

from FACTS ABOUT THE MOON

from THE BOOK OF MEN

ONLY AS THE DAY IS LONG: NEW POEMS

from

AWAKE

Two Pictures of My Sister

If an ordinary person is silent,
this may be a tactical maneuver.
If a writer is silent, he is lying.

—JAROSLAV SEIFERT

The pose is stolen from Monroe, struck
in the sun's floodlight, eyes lowered,
a long-stemmed plastic rose between her teeth.
My cast-off bathing suit hangs
in folds over her ribs, straps
cinched, pinned at the back of her neck.
Barefoot on the hot cement, knock-kneed,
comical if it weren't for the graceful
angles of her arms, her flesh soft
against the chipped stucco.

The other picture is in my head.
It is years later.
It is in color.
Blonde hair curls away from the planes of her face
like wood shavings.
She wears a lemon-yellow ruffled top, denim
cutoffs, her belly button squeezed to a slit
above the silver snap.
She stands against the hallway wall
while Dad shakes his belt in her face.
A strip of skin has been peeled
from her bare shoulder, there are snake
lines across her thighs, a perfect curl
around her long neck.
She looks through him
as if she could see behind his head.

She dares him.
Go on. Hit me again.
He lets the folded strap unravel to the floor.
Holds it by its tail. Bells the buckle
off her cheekbone.
She does not move or cry or even wince
as the welt blooms on her temple
like a flower opening frame by frame
in a nature film.
It lowers her eyelid with its violet petals
and as he walks away only her eyes
move, like the eyes of a portrait that follow you
around a museum room, her face
a stubborn moon that trails the car all night,
stays locked in the frame of the back window
no matter how many turns you take,
no matter how far you go.

What My Father Told Me

Always I have done what was asked.
Melmac dishes stacked on rag towels.
The slack of a vacuum cleaner cord
wound around my hand. Laundry
hung on a line.
There is always much to do and I do it.
The iron resting in its frame, hot
in the shallow pan of summer
as the basins of his hands push
aside the book I am reading.
I do as I am told, hold his penis
like the garden hose, in this bedroom,
in that bathroom, over the toilet
or my bare stomach.
I do the chores, pull the weeds out back,
finger stink-bug husks, snail carcasses,
pile dead grass in black bags. At night
his feet are safe on their pads, light
on the wall-to-wall as he takes
the hallway to my room.
His voice, the hiss of the lawn sprinklers,
the wet hush of sweat in his hollows,
the mucus still damp
in the corners of my eyes as I wake.

Summer ends. Schoolwork doesn't suit me.
My fingers unaccustomed to the slimness
of a pen, the delicate touch it takes
to uncoil the mind.
History. A dateline pinned to the wall.
Beneath each president's face, a quotation.

Pictures of buffalo and wheat fields,
a wagon train circled for the night,
my hand raised to ask a question,
Where did the children sleep?

Ghosts

It's midnight and a light rain falls.
I sit on the front stoop to smoke.
Across the street a lit window, filled
with a ladder on which a young man stands.
His head dips into the frame each time
he sinks his brush in the paint.

He's painting his kitchen white, patiently
covering the faded yellow with long strokes.
He leans into this work like a lover, risks
losing his balance, returns gracefully
to the precise middle of the step to dip
and start again.

A woman appears beneath his feet, borrows
paint, takes it onto her thin brush
like a tongue. Her sweater is the color
of tender lemons. This is the beginning
of their love, bare and simple
as that wet room.

My hip aches against the damp cement.
I take it inside, punch up a pillow
for it to nest in. I'm getting too old
to sit on the porch in the rain,
to stay up all night, watch morning
rise over rooftops.

                    Too old to dance
circles in dirty bars, a man's hands
laced at the small of my spine, pink
slingbacks hung from limp fingers. Love.

I'm too old for that, the foreign tongues
loose in my mouth, teeth that rang
my breasts by the nipples like soft bells.

I want it back. The red earrings and blue
slips. Lips alive with spit. Muscles
twisting like boat ropes in a hard wind.
Bellies for pillows. Not this ache in my hip.

I want the girl who cut through blue poolrooms
of smoke and golden beers, stepping out alone
into a summer fog to stand beneath a streetlamp's
amber halo, her blue palms cupped
around the flare of a match.

She could have had so many lives. Gone off
with a boy to Arizona, lived on a ranch
under waves of carved rock, her hands turned
the color of flat red sands. Could have said
yes to a woman with fingers tapered as candles,
or a man who slept in a canvas tepee, who pulled
her down on his mattress of grass where she made
herself as empty as the guttered fire.

                              Oklahoma.
I could be there now, spinning corn from dry cobs,
working fat tomatoes into mason jars.

The rain has stopped. For blocks the houses
drip like ticking clocks. I turn off lights
and feel my way to the bedroom, slip cold
toes between flowered sheets, nest my chest
into the back of a man who sleeps in fits,
his suits hung stiff in the closet, his racked
shoes tipped toward the ceiling.

This man loves me for my wit, my nerve,
for the way my long legs fall from hemmed skirts.
When he rolls his body against mine, I know
he feels someone else. There's no blame.
I love him, even as I remember a man with cane-
brown hands, palms pink as blossoms opening
over my breasts.

                    And he holds me,
even with all those other fingers nestled
inside me, even with all those other shoulders
wedged above his own like wings.

The Garden

We were talking about poetry.
We were talking about nuclear war.
She said she couldn't write about it
because she couldn't imagine it.
I said it was simple. Imagine
this doorknob is the last thing
you will see in this world.
Imagine you happen to be standing
at the door when you look down, about
to grasp the knob, your fingers
curled toward it, the doorknob old
and black with oil from being turned
so often in your hand, cranky
with rust and grease from the kitchen.
Imagine it happens this quickly, before
you have time to think of anything else;
your kids, your own life, what it will mean.
You reach for the knob and the window
flares white, though you see it only
from the corner of your eye because
you're looking at the knob, intent
on opening the back door to the patch
of sunlight on the porch, that garden
spread below the stairs and the single
tomato you might pick for a salad.
But when the flash comes you haven't
thought that far ahead. It is only
the simple desire to move into the sun
that possesses you. The thought
of the garden, that tomato, would have
come after you had taken the knob
in your hand, just beginning to twist it,

and when the window turns white
you are only about to touch it,
preparing to open the door.

The Tooth Fairy

They brushed a quarter with glue
and glitter, slipped in on bare
feet, and without waking me
painted rows of delicate gold
footprints on my sheets with a love
so quiet, I still can't hear it.

My mother must have been
a beauty then, sitting
at the kitchen table with him,
a warm breeze lifting her
embroidered curtains, waiting
for me to fall asleep.

It's harder to believe
the years that followed, the palms
curled into fists, a floor
of broken dishes, her chain-smoking
through long silences, him
punching holes in the walls.

I can still remember her print
dresses, his checkered taxi, the day
I found her in the closet
with a paring knife, the night
he kicked my sister in the ribs.

He lives alone in Oregon now, dying
slowly of a rare bone disease.
His face stippled gray, his ankles
clotted beneath wool socks.

She's a nurse on the graveyard shift.
Comes home mornings and calls me.
Drinks her dark beer and goes to bed.

And I still wonder how they did it, slipped
that quarter under my pillow, made those
perfect footprints . . .

Whenever I visit her, I ask again.
"I don't know," she says, rocking, closing
her eyes. "We were as surprised as you."

and the house swept with the colors of dusk,
I set the table with plates and lace. In these minutes
left to myself, before the man and child scuff at the doorstep
and come in, I think of you and wonder what I would say
if I could write. Would I tell you how I avoid his eyes,
this man I've learned to live with, afraid
of what he doesn't know about me. That I've finished
a pack of cigarettes in one sitting, to ready myself
for dinner, when my hands will waver over a plate of fish
as my daughter grows up normal in the chair beside me. Missy,

this is what's become of the wedding you swore you'd come to
wearing black. That was in 1970 as we sat on the bleached
floor of the sanitarium sharing a cigarette you'd won
in a game of pool. You said even school was better
than this ward, where they placed the old men
in their draped pants, the housewives screaming in loud
flowered shifts as they clung to the doors that lined the halls.
When we ate our dinner of fish and boiled potatoes,
it was you who nudged me under the table
as the thin man in striped pajamas climbed
the chair beside me in his bare feet, his pink-tinged urine
making soup of my leftovers. With my eyes locked on yours,
I watched you keep eating. So I lifted my fork
to my open mouth, jello quivering green
against the tines, and while I trusted you and chewed
on nothing, he leapt into the arms of the night nurse
and bit open the side of her face. You had been there

longer, knew the ropes, how to take the sugar-coated pill
and slip it into the side pocket in your mouth, pretend
to swallow it down in drowsy gulps while

the white-frocked nurse eyed the clockface above our heads.
You tapped messages into the wall while I wept, struggling
to remember the code, snuck in after bedcount
with cigarettes, blew the blue smoke through barred windows.
We traded stories, our military fathers:
yours locking you in a closet for the days it took
to chew ribbons of flesh from your fingers, a coat
pulled over your head; mine, who worked
his ringed fingers inside me while the house
slept, my face pressed to the pillow, my fists
knotted into the sheets. Some nights

I can't eat. The dining room fills
with their chatter, my hand stuffed with the glint
of a fork and the safety of butter knives
quiet at the sides of our plates. If I could write you now,
I'd tell you I wonder how long I can go on with this careful
pouring of the wine from the bottle, straining to catch it
in the fragile glass. Tearing open my bread, I see

the scar, stitches laced up the root of your arm, the flesh messy
where you grabbed at it with the broken glass of an ashtray.
That was the third time. And later you laughed
when they twisted you into the white strapped jacket
demanding you vomit the pills. I imagined you
in the harsh light of a bare bulb where you took
the needle without flinching, retched
when the ipecac hit you, your body shelved over
the toilet and no one to hold the hair
from your face. I don't know

where your hands are now, the fingers that filled my mouth
those nights you tongued me open in the broken light
that fell through chicken-wired windows. The intern
found us and wrenched us apart, the half-moon of your breast

exposed as you spit on him. "Now you're going to get it,"
he hissed through this teeth and you screamed, "Get what?"
As if there was anything anyone could give you.
If I could write you now, I'd tell you

I still see your face, bone-white as my china
above the black velvet cape you wore to my wedding
twelve years ago, the hem of your black crepe skirt
brushing up the dirty rice in swirls
as you swept down the reception line to kiss me.
"Now you're going to get it," you whispered,
cupping my cheek in your hand.

Awake

Except for the rise and fall of a thin sheet
draped across your chest, you could be dead.
Your hair curled into the pillow.
Arms flung wide. The moon fills our window
and I stand in a white
rectangle of light. Hands crossed
over empty breasts. In an hour
the moon will lower itself. In the backyard
the dog will bark, dig up his bone
near the redwood fence. If we could have had
children, or religion, maybe sleep
wouldn't feel like death, like shovel heads
packing the black earth down.
Morning will come because it has to.
You will open your eyes. The sun
will flare and rise. Chisel the hills
into shape. The sax player next door
will lift his horn and pour
music over the downturned Vs of rooftops,
the tangled ivy, the shivering tree,
giving it all back to us as he breathes:
The garden. The hard blue sky. The sweet
apple of light.

Girl in the Doorway

She is twelve now, the door to her room
closed, telephone cord trailing the hallway
in tight curls. I stand at the dryer, listening
through the thin wall between us, her voice
rising and falling as she describes her new life.
Static flies in brief blue stars from her socks,
her hairbrush in the morning. Her silver braces
shine inside the velvet case of her mouth.
Her grades rise and fall, her friends call
or they don't, her dog chews her new shoes
to a canvas pulp. Some days she opens her door
and musk rises from the long crease in her bed,
fills the dim hall. She grabs a denim coat
and drags the floor. Dust swirls in gold eddies
behind her. She walks through the house, a goddess,
each window pulsing with summer. Outside,
the boys wait for her teeth to straighten.
They have a vibrant patience.
When she steps onto the front porch, sun shimmies
through the tips of her hair, the V of her legs,
fans out like wings under her arms
as she raises them and waves. Goodbye, Goodbye.
Then she turns to go, folds up
all that light in her arms like a blanket
and takes it with her.

The cat calls for her dinner.
On the porch I bend and pour
brown soy stars into her bowl,
stroke her dark fur.
It's not quite night.
Pinpricks of light in the eastern sky.
Above my neighbor's roof, a transparent
moon, a pink rag of cloud.
Inside my house are those who love me.
My daughter dusts biscuit dough.
And there's a man who will lift my hair
in his hands, brush it
until it throws sparks.
Everything is just as I've left it.
Dinner simmers on the stove.
Glass bowls wait to be filled
with gold broth. Sprigs of parsley
on the cutting board.
I want to smell this rich soup, the air
around me going dark, as stars press
their simple shapes into the sky.
I want to stay on the back porch
while the world tilts
toward sleep, until what I love
misses me, and calls me in.

Bird

For days now a red-breasted bird
has been trying to break in.
She tests a low branch, violet blossoms
swaying beside her, leaps into the air and flies
straight at my window, beak and breast
held back, claws raking the pane.
Maybe she longs for the tree she sees
reflected in the glass, but I'm only guessing.
I watch until she gives up and swoops off.
I wait for her return, the familiar
click, swoosh, thump of her. I sip cold coffee
and scan the room, trying to see it new,
through the eyes of a bird. Nothing has changed.
Books piled in a corner, coats hooked
over chair backs, paper plates, a cup
half-filled with sour milk.
The children are in school. The man is at work.
I'm alone with dead roses in a jam jar.
What do I have that she could want enough
to risk such failure, again and again?

The Laundromat

My clothes somersault in the dryer. At thirty
I float in and out of a new kind of horniness,
the kind where you get off on words and gestures;
long talks about art are foreplay, the climax
is watching a man eat a Napoleon while he drives.
Across from me a fifty-year-old matron folds clothes,
her eyes focused on the nipples of a young man in
silk jogging shorts. He looks up, catching her.
She giggles and blurts out, "Hot, isn't it?"
A man on my right eyes the line of my shorts, waiting
for me to bend over. I do. An act of animal kindness.
A long black jogger swings in off the street to
splash his face in the sink and I watch the room
become a sweet humid jungle. We crowd around
the Amazon at the watering hole, twitching our noses
like wildebeests or buffalo, snorting, rooting out
mates in the heat. I want to hump every moving thing
in this place. I want to lie down in the dry dung
and dust and twist to scratch my back. I want to
stretch and prowl and grow lazy in the shade. I want
to have a slew of cubs. "Do you have change for
a quarter?" he asks, scratching the inside of his thigh.
Back in the Laundromat my socks are sticking to my
sheets. Caught in the crackle of static electricity,
I fold my underwear. I notice the honey-colored
stains in each silk crotch. Odd-shaped, like dreams,
I make my panties into neat squares and drop them,
smiling, into the wicker basket.

Sunday

We sit on the lawn, an Igloo
cooler between us. So hot, the sky
is white. Above gravel rooftops
a spire, a shimmering cross.

You pick up the swollen hose, press
your thick thumb into the silver nozzle.
A fan of water sprays rainbows
over the dying lawn. Hummingbirds

sparkle green. Bellies powdered
with pollen from the bottle-brush tree.
The bells of twelve o'clock.
Our neighbors return from church.

I bow my head as they ease
clean cars into neat garages, file
through screen doors in lace gloves,
white hats, Bible-black suits.

The smell of barbeque rises, hellish
thick and sweet. I envy their weekly
peace of mind. They know
where they're going when they die.

Charcoal fluid cans contract in the sun.
I want to be Catholic. A Jew. Maybe
a Methodist. I want to kneel
for days on rough wood.

Their kids appear in bright shorts,
bathing suits, their rubber thongs

flapping down the hot cement.
They could be anyone's children;

they have God inside their tiny bodies.
My god, look how they float, like birds
through the scissor-scissor-scissor
of lawn sprinklers.

Down the street, a tinny radio bleats.
The sun bulges above our house
like an eye. I don't want to die.
I never want to leave this block.

I envy everything, all of it. I know
it's a sin. I love how you can shift
in your chair, take a deep drink
of gold beer, curl your toes under, and hum.

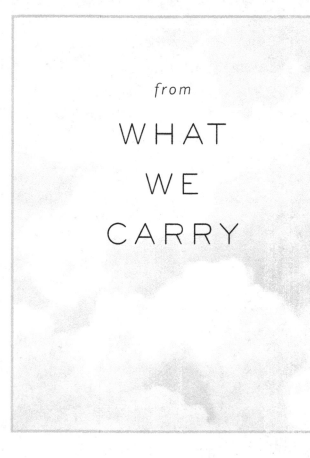

from

WHAT
WE
CARRY

Late October

Midnight. The cats under the open window,
their guttural, territorial yowls.

Crouched in the neighbor's driveway with a broom,
I jab at them with the bristle end,

chasing their raised tails as they scramble
from bush to bush, intent on killing each other.

I shout and kick until they finally
give it up; one shimmies beneath the fence,

the other under a car. I stand in my underwear
in the trembling quiet, remembering my dream.

Something had been stolen from me, valueless
and irreplaceable. Grease and grass blades

were stuck to the bottoms of my feet.
I was shaking and sweating. I had wanted

to *kill* them. The moon was a white dinner plate
broken exactly in half. I saw myself as I was:

forty-one years old, standing on a slab
of cold concrete, a broom handle slipping

from my hands, my breasts bare, my hair
on end, afraid of what I might do next.

After Twelve Days of Rain

I couldn't name it, the sweet
sadness welling up in me for weeks.
So I cleaned, found myself standing
in a room with a rag in my hand,
the birds calling *time-to-go, time-to-go.*
And like an old woman near the end
of her life I could hear it, the voice
of a man I never loved who pressed
my breasts to his lips and whispered
"My little doves, my white, white lilies."
I could almost cry when I remember it.

I don't remember when I began
to call everyone "sweetie,"
as if they were my daughters,
my darlings, my little birds.
I have always loved too much,
or not enough. Last night
I read a poem about God and almost
believed it—God sipping coffee,
smoking cherry tobacco. I've arrived
at a time in my life when I could believe
almost anything.

Today, pumping gas into my old car, I stood
hatless in the rain and the whole world
went silent—cars on the wet street
sliding past without sound, the attendant's
mouth opening and closing on air
as he walked from pump to pump, his footsteps
erased in the rain—nothing
but the tiny numbers in their square windows

rolling by my shoulder, the unstoppable seconds
gliding by as I stood at the Chevron,
balanced evenly on my two feet, a gas nozzle
gripped in my hand, my hair gathering rain.

And I saw it didn't matter
who had loved me or who I loved. I was alone.
The black oily asphalt, the slick beauty
of the Iranian attendant, the thickening
clouds—nothing was mine. And I understood
finally, after a semester of philosophy,
a thousand books of poetry, after death
and childbirth and the startled cries of men
who called out my name as they entered me,
I finally believed I was alone, felt it
in my actual, visceral heart, heard it echo
like a thin bell. And the sounds
came back, the *slish* of tires
and footsteps, all the delicate cargo
they carried saying thank you
and yes. So I paid and climbed into my car
as if nothing had happened—
as if everything mattered—What else could I do?

I drove to the grocery store
and bought wheat bread and milk,
a candy bar wrapped in gold foil,
smiled at the teenaged cashier
with the pimpled face and the plastic
name plate pinned above her small breast,
and knew her secret, her sweet fear—
Little bird. Little darling. She handed me
my change, my brown bag, a torn receipt,
pushed the cash drawer in with her hip
and smiled back.

Aphasia

for Honeya

After the stroke all she could say
was *Venezuela*, pointing to the pitcher
with its bright blue rim, her one word
command. And when she drank the clear
water in and gave the glass back,
it was *Venezuela* again, gratitude,
maybe, or the word now simply
a sigh, like the sky in the window,
the pillows a cloudy definition
propped beneath her head. Pink roses
dying on the bedside table, each fallen
petal a scrap in the shape of a country
she'd never been to, had never once
expressed interest in, and now
it was everywhere, in the peach
she lifted, dripping, to her lips,
the white tissue in the box, her brooding
children when they came to visit,
baptized with their new name
after each kiss. And at night
she whispered it, dark narcotic
in her husband's ear as he bent
to listen, her hands, fumbling
at her buttons, her breasts,
holding them up to the light
like a gift. *Venezuela*, she said.

What We Carry

for Donald

He tells me his mother carries his father's ashes
on the front seat in a cardboard box, exactly
where she placed them after the funeral.
Her explanation: she hasn't decided
where they should be scattered.
It's been three years.
I imagine her driving home from the store,
a sack of groceries jostling next to the box—
smell of lemons, breakfast rolls,
the radio tuned to the news.
He says he never liked his father,
but made peace with him before he died.
That he carries what he can
and discards the rest.
We are sitting in a café.
Because I don't love him, I love
to watch him watch the women walk by
in their sheer summer skirts.
From where I sit I can see them approach,
then study his face as he watches them go.
We are friends. We are both lonely.
I never tell him about my father
so he doesn't know that when I think of his—
blue ashes in a cardboard box—I think
of my own, alive in a room
somewhere in Oregon, a woman
helping his worn body into bed, the same body
that crushed my sister's childhood, mine.
Maybe this wife kisses him
goodnight, tells him she loves him,
actually means it. This close to the end,

if he asked forgiveness, what could I say?
If I were handed my father's ashes,
what would I do with them?
What body of water would be fit
for his scattering? What ground?
It's best when I think least. I listen
to my friend's story without judgment
or surprise, taking it in as he takes in
the women, without question, simply a given,
as unexceptional as conversation between friends,
the laughter, and at each end
the relative comfort of silence.

For the Sake of Strangers

No matter what the grief, its weight,
we are obliged to carry it.
We rise and gather momentum, the dull strength
that pushes us through crowds.
And then the young boy gives me directions
so avidly. A woman holds the glass door open,
waits patiently for my empty body to pass through.
All day it continues, each kindness
reaching toward another—a stranger
singing to no one as I pass on the path, trees
offering their blossoms, a Down child
who lifts his almond eyes and smiles.
Somehow they always find me, seem even
to be waiting, determined to keep me
from myself, from the thing that calls to me
as it must have once called to them—
this temptation to step off the edge
and fall weightless, away from the world.

Dust

Someone spoke to me last night,
told me the truth. Just a few words,
but I recognized it.
I knew I should make myself get up,
write it down, but it was late,
and I was exhausted from working
all day in the garden, moving rocks.
Now, I remember only the flavor—
not like food, sweet or sharp.
More like a fine powder, like dust.
And I wasn't elated or frightened,
but simply rapt, aware.
That's how it is sometimes—
God comes to your window,
all bright light and black wings,
and you're just too tired to open it.

Twelve

Deep in the canyon, under the red branches
of a manzanita, we turned the pages
slowly, seriously, as if it were a holy text,
just as the summer before we had turned
the dark undersides of rocks to interrupt
the lives of ants, or a black stink bug
and her hard-backed brood.
And because the boys always came,
even though they weren't invited, we never
said anything, except Brenda who whispered
Turn the page when she thought we'd seen enough.
This went on for weeks one summer, a few of us
meeting at the canyon rim at noon, the glossy
magazine fluttering at the tips of our fingers.
Brenda led the way down, and the others
stumbled after blindly, Martin,
always with his little brother
hanging off the pocket of his jeans, a blue
pacifier stuck like candy in his mouth.
Every time he yawned, the wet nipple
fell out into the dirt, and Martin, the good brother,
would pick it up, dust it with the underside
of his shirt, then slip it into his own mouth
and suck it clean. And when the turning
of the pages began, ceremoniously, exposing
thigh after thigh, breast after beautiful, terrible
breast, Martin leaned to one side,
and slid the soft palm of his hand
over his baby brother's eyes.

Each Sound

Beginnings are brutal, like this accident
of stars colliding, mute explosions
of colorful gases, the mist and dust
that would become our bodies
hurling through black holes, rising,
muck-ridden, from pits of tar and clay.
Back then it was easy to have teeth,
claw our way into the trees—it was
accepted, the monkeys loved us, sat
on their red asses clapping and laughing.
We've forgotten the luxury of dumbness,
how once we crouched naked on an outcrop
of rock, the moon huge and untouched
above us, speechless. Now we talk
about everything, incessantly,
our moans and grunts turned on a spit
into warm vowels and elegant consonants.
We say *plethora, demitasse, ozone* and *love.*
We think we know what each sound means.
There are times when something so joyous
or so horrible happens our only response
is an intake of breath, and then
we're back at the truth of it,
that ball of life expanding
and exploding on impact, our heads,
our chests, filled with that first
unspeakable light.

Fast Gas

for Richard

Before the day of self service,
when you never had to pump your own gas,
I was the one who did it for you, the girl
who stepped out at the sound of a bell
with a blue rag in my hand, my hair pulled back
in a straight, unlovely ponytail.
This was before automatic shut-offs
and vapor seals, and once, while filling a tank,
I hit a bubble of trapped air and the gas
backed up, came arcing out of the hole
in a bright gold wave and soaked me—face, breasts,
belly and legs. And I had to hurry
back to the booth, the small employee bathroom
with the broken lock, to change my uniform,
peel the gas-soaked cloth from my skin
and wash myself in the sink.
Light-headed, scrubbed raw, I felt
pure and amazed—the way the amber gas
glazed my flesh, the searing,
subterranean pain of it, how my skin
shimmered and ached, glowed
like rainbowed oil on the pavement.
I was twenty. In a few weeks I would fall,
for the first time, in love, that man waiting
patiently in my future like a red leaf
on the sidewalk, the kind of beauty
that asks to be noticed. How was I to know
it would begin this way: every cell of my body
burning with a dangerous beauty, the air around me
a nimbus of light that would carry me
through the days, how when he found me

weeks later, he would find me like that,
an ordinary woman who could rise
in flame, all he would have to do
is come close and touch me.

As It Is

The man I love hates technology, hates
that he's forced to use it: telephones
and microfilm, air conditioning,
car radios and the occasional fax.
He wishes he lived in the old world,
sitting on a stump carving a clothespin
or a spoon. He wants to go back, slip
like lint into his great-great-grandfather's
pocket, reborn as a pilgrim, a peasant,
a dirt farmer hoeing his uneven rows.
He walks when he can, through the hills
behind his house, his dogs panting beside him
like small steam engines. He's delighted
by the sun's slow and simple
descent, the complicated machinery
of his own body. I would have loved him
in any era, in any dark age, I would take him
into the twilight and unwind him, slide
my fingers through his hair and pull him
to his knees. As it is, this afternoon, late
in the twentieth century, I sit on a chair
in the kitchen with my keys in my lap, pressing
the black button on the answering machine
over and over, listening to his message,
his voice strung along the wires outside my window
where the birds balance themselves
and stare off into the trees, thinking
even in the farthest future, in the most
distant universe, I would have recognized
this voice, refracted, as it would be, like light
from some small, uncharted star.

The Thief

What is it when your man sits on the floor
in sweatpants, his latest project
set out in front of him like a small world, maps
and photographs, diagrams and plans, everything
he hopes to build, invent or create,
and you believe in him as you always have,
even after the failures, even more now
as you set your coffee down
and move toward him, to where he sits
oblivious of you, concentrating
in a square of sun—
you step over the rulers and blue graph-paper
to squat behind him, and he barely notices
though you're still in your robe
which falls open a little as you reach
around his chest, feel for the pink
wheel of each nipple, the slow beat
of his heart, your ear pressed to his back
to listen—and you are torn,
not wanting to interrupt his work
but unable to keep your fingers
from dipping into the ditch in his pants,
torn again with tenderness
for the way his flesh grows unwillingly
toward your curved palm, toward the light,
as if you had planted it, this sweet root,
your mouth already an echo of its shape—
you slip your tongue into his ear
and he hears you, calling him away
from his work, the angled lines of his thoughts,
into the shapeless place you are bound
to take him, over bridges of bone, beyond

borders of skin, climbing over him
into the world of the body, its labyrinth
of ladders and stairs—and you love him
like the first time you loved him,
with equal measures of expectancy
and fear and awe, taking him with you
into the soft geometry of the flesh, the earth
before its sidewalks and cities,
its glistening spires,
stealing him back from the world he loves
into this other world he cannot build without you.

This Close

In the room where we lie, light
stains the drawn shades yellow.
We sweat and pull at each other, climb
with our fingers the slippery ladders of rib.
Wherever our bodies touch, the flesh
comes alive. Heat and need, like invisible
animals, gnaw at my breasts, the soft
insides of your thighs. What I want
I simply reach out and take, no delicacy now,
the dark human bread I eat handful
by greedy handful. Eyes, fingers, mouths,
sweet leeches of desire. Crazy woman,
her brain full of bees, see how her palms curl
into fists and beat the pillow senseless.
And when my body finally gives in to it
then pulls itself away, salt-laced
and arched with its final ache, I am
so grateful I would give you anything, anything.
If I loved you, being this close would kill me.

The Lovers

She is about to come. This time,
they are sitting up, joined below the belly,
feet cupped like sleek hands praying
at the base of each other's spines.
And when something lifts within her
toward a light she's sure, once again,
she can't bear, she opens her eyes
and sees his face is turned away,
one arm behind him, hand splayed
palm down on the mattress, to brace himself
so he can lever his hips, touch
with the bright tip the innermost spot.
And she finds she *can't* bear it—
not his beautiful neck, stretched and corded,
not his hair fallen to one side like beach grass,
not the curved wing of his ear, washed thin
with daylight, deep pink of the inner body.
What she can't bear is that she can't see his face,
not that she thinks this exactly—she is rocking
and breathing—it's more her body's thought,
opening, as it is, into its own sheer truth.
So that when her hand lifts of its own volition
and slaps him, twice on the chest,
on that pad of muscled flesh just above the nipple,
slaps him twice, fast, like a nursing child
trying to get a mother's attention,
she's startled by the sound,
though when he turns his face to hers—
which is what her body wants, his eyes
pulled open, as if she had bitten—
she does reach out and bite him, on the shoulder,
not hard, but with the power infants have

over those who have borne them, tied as they are
to the body, and so, tied to the pleasure,
the exquisite pain of this world.
And when she lifts her face he sees
where she's gone, knows she can't speak,
is traveling toward something essential,
toward the core of her need, so he simply
watches, steadily, with an animal calm
as she arches and screams, watches the face that,
if she could see it, she would never let him see.

Kissing

They are kissing, on a park bench,
on the edge of an old bed, in a doorway
or on the floor of a church. Kissing
as the streets fill with balloons
or soldiers, locusts or confetti, water
or fire or dust. Kissing down through
the centuries under sun or stars, a dead tree,
an umbrella, amid derelicts. Kissing
as Christ carries his cross, as Gandhi
sings his speeches, as a bullet
careens through the air toward a child's
good heart. They are kissing,
long, deep, spacious kisses, exploring
the silence of the tongue, the mute
rungs of the upper palate, hungry
for the living flesh. They are still
kissing when the cars crash and the bombs
drop, when the babies are born crying
into the white air, when Mozart bends
to his bowl of soup and Stalin
bends to his garden. They are kissing
to begin the world again. Nothing
can stop them. They kiss until their lips
swell, their thick tongues quickening
to the budded touch, licking up
the sweet juices. I want to believe
they are kissing to save the world,
but they're not. All they know
is this press and need, these two-legged
beasts, their faces like roses crushed
together and opening, they are covering
their teeth, they are doing what they have to do

to survive the worst, they are sealing
the hard words in, they are dying
for our sins. In a broken world they are
practicing this simple and singular act
to perfection. They are holding
onto each other. They are kissing.

from

SMOKE

Death Comes to Me Again, a Girl

Death comes to me again, a girl in a cotton slip.
Barefoot, giggling. It's not so terrible, she tells me,
not like you think: all darkness and silence.

There are wind chimes and the scent of lemons.
Some days it rains. But more often the air
is dry and sweet. We sit beneath the staircase
built from hair and bone and listen
to the voices of the living.

I like it, she says, shaking the dust from her hair.
Especially when they fight, and when they sing.

How It Will Happen, When

There you are, exhausted from a night of crying, curled up on the couch,
the floor, at the foot of the bed, anywhere you fall you fall down crying,
half amazed at what the body is capable of, not believing you can cry
anymore. And there they are, his socks, his shirt, your underwear
and your winter gloves, all in a loose pile next to the bathroom door,
and you fall down again. Someday, years from now, things will be
different, the house clean for once, everything in its place, windows
shining, sun coming in easily now, sliding across the high shine of wax
on the wood floor. You'll be peeling an orange or watching a bird
spring from the edge of the rooftop next door, noticing how,
for an instant, its body is stopped on the air, only a moment before
gathering the will to fly into the ruff at its wings and then doing it:
flying. You'll be reading, and for a moment there will be a word
you don't understand, a simple word like *now* or *what* or *is*
and you'll ponder over it like a child discovering language.
Is you'll say over and over until it begins to make sense, and that's
when you'll say it, for the first time, out loud: He's dead. He's not
coming back. And it will be the first time you believe it.

Fear

We were afraid of everything: earthquakes,
strangers, smoke above the canyon, the fire
that would come running and eat up our house,
the Claymore girls, big-boned, rough, razor blades
tucked in their ratted hair. We were terrified

of polio, tuberculosis, being found out, the tent
full of boys two blocks over, the kick ball, the asphalt,
the pain-filled rocks, the glass-littered canyon, the deep
cave gouged in its side, the wheelbarrow crammed
with dirty magazines, beer cans, spit-laced butts.

We were afraid of hands, screen doors slammed
by angry mothers, abandoned cars, their slumped
back seats, the chain-link fence we couldn't climb
fast enough, electrical storms, blackouts, fistfights
behind the pancake house, Original Sin, sidewalk
cracks and the corner crematorium, loose brakes
on the handlebars of our bikes. It came alive

behind our eyes: ant mounds, wasp nests, the bird
half-eaten on the scratchy grass, chained dogs,
the boggy creek bed, the sewer main that fed it,
the game where you had to hold your breath
until you passed out. We were afraid of being

poor, dumb, yelled at, ignored, invisible
as the nuclear dust we were told to wipe
from lids before we opened them in the kitchen,
the fat roll of meat that slid into the pot, sleep,
dreams, the soundless swing of the father's ringed
fist, the mother's face turned away, the wet bed,

anything red, wrenches left scattered in the dirt,
the slow leak, the stain on the driveway, oily gears
soaking in a shallow pan, busted chairs stuffed
in the rafters of the neighbor's garage, the Chevy's
twisted undersides jacked up on blocks.

It was what we knew best, understood least,
it whipped through our bodies like fire or sleet.
We were lured by the dumpster behind the liquor store,
fissures in the baked earth, the smell of singed hair,
the brassy hum of high-tension towers, train tracks,
buzzards over a ditch, black widows, the cat
with one eye, the red spot on the back of the skirt,
the fallout shelter's metal door hinged to the rusty
grass, the back way, the wrong path, the night's
wide back, the coiled bedsprings of the sister's top
bunk, the wheezing, the cousin in the next room
tapping on the wall, anything small.

We were afraid of clothesline, curtain rods, the worn
hairbrush, the good-for-nothings we were about to become,
reform school, the long ride to the ocean on the bus,
the man at the back of the bus, the underpass.

We were afraid of fingers of pickleweed crawling
over the embankment, the French Kiss, the profound
silence of dead fish, burning sand, rotting elastic
in the waistbands of our underpants, jellyfish, riptides,
eucalyptus bark unraveling, the pink flesh beneath,
the stink of seaweed, seagulls landing near our feet,
their hateful eyes, their orange-tipped beaks stabbing
the sand, the crumbling edge of the continent we stood on,
waiting to be saved, the endless, wind-driven waves.

Last Words

for Al

His voice, toward the end, was a soft coal breaking
open in the little stove of his heart. One day
he just let go and the birds stopped singing.

Then the other deaths came on, as if by permission—
beloved teacher, cousin, a lover slipped from my life
the way a rope slithers from your grip, the ocean
folding over it, your fingers stripped of flesh. A deck

of cards, worn smooth at a kitchen table, the jack
of spades laid down at last, his face thumbed to threads.
An ashtray full of pebbles on the window ledge, wave-beaten,
gathered at day's end from a beach your mind has never left,

then a starling climbs the pine outside—
the cat's black paw, the past shattered, the stones
rolled to their forever-hidden places. Even the poets

I had taken to my soul: Levis, Matthews, Levertov—
the books of poetry, lost or stolen, left on airport benches,
shabby trade paperbacks of my childhood, the box
misplaced, the one suitcase that mattered crushed

to nothing in the belly of a train. I took a rubbing
of the carved wings and lilies from a headstone
outside Philadelphia, frosted gin bottles
stationed like soldiers on her grave:

The Best Blues Singer in the World
Will Never Stop Singing.

How many losses does it take to stop a heart,
to lay waste to the vocabularies of desire?
Each one came rushing through the rooms he left.
Mouths open. Last words flown up into the trees.

Trying to Raise the Dead

Look at me. I'm standing on a deck
in the middle of Oregon. There are
people inside the house, It's not my

house, you don't know them.
They're drinking and singing
and playing guitars. You love

this song. Remember? "Ophelia."
Boards on the windows, mail
by the door. I'm whispering

so they won't think I'm crazy.
They don't know me that well.
Where are you now? I feel stupid.

I'm talking to trees, to leaves
swarming on the black air, stars
blinking in and out of heart-

shaped shadows, to the moon, half-
lit and barren, stuck like an ax
between the branches. What are you

now? Air? Mist? Dust? Light?
What? Give me something. I have
to know where to send my voice.

A direction. An object. My love, it needs
a place to rest. Say anything. I'm listening.
I'm ready to believe. Even lies, I don't care.

Say *burning bush*. Say *stone*. They've
stopped singing now and I really should go.
So tell me, quickly. It's April. I'm

on Spring Street. That's my gray car
in the driveway. They're laughing
and dancing. Someone's bound

to show up soon. I'm waving.
Give me a sign if you can see me.
I'm the only one here on my knees.

The Shipfitter's Wife

I loved him most
when he came home from work,
his fingers still curled from fitting pipe,
his denim shirt ringed with sweat,
smelling of salt, the drying weeds
of the ocean. I'd go to where he sat
on the edge of the bed, his forehead
anointed with grease, his cracked hands
jammed between his thighs, and unlace
the steel-toed boots, stroke his ankles
and calves, the pads and bones of his feet.
Then I'd open his clothes and take
the whole day inside me—the ship's
gray sides, the miles of copper pipe,
the voice of the foreman clanging
off the hull's silver ribs. Spark of lead
kissing metal. The clamp, the winch,
the white fire of the torch, the whistle,
and the long drive home.

Abschied Symphony

Someone I love is dying, which is why,
when I turn the key in the ignition
and the radio comes on, sudden and loud,
something by Haydn, a diminishing fugue,
then back the car out of the parking space
in the underground garage, maneuvering through
the dimly lit tunnels, under low ceilings,
following yellow arrows stenciled at intervals
on gray cement walls and I think of him,
moving slowly through the last
hard days of his life, I won't
turn it off, and I can't stop crying.
When I arrive at the tollgate I have to make
myself stop thinking as I dig in my pockets
for the last of my coins, turn to the attendant,
indifferent in his blue smock, his white hair
curling like smoke around his weathered neck,
and say *Thank you*, like an idiot, and drive
into the blinding midday light.
Everything is hideously symbolic:
the Chevron truck, its underbelly
spattered with road grit and the sweat
of last night's rain, the dumpster
behind the flower shop, sprung lid
pressed down on dead wedding bouquets—
even the smell of something simple, coffee
drifting from the open door of a café,
and my eyes glaze over, ache in their sockets.
For months now all I've wanted is the blessing
of inattention, to move carefully from room to room
in my small house, numb with forgetfulness.
To eat a bowl of cereal and not imagine him,

drawn thin and pale, unable to swallow.
How not to imagine the tumors
ripening beneath his skin, flesh
I have kissed, stroked with my fingertips,
pressed my belly and breasts against, some nights
so hard I thought I could enter him, open
his back at the spine like a door or a curtain
and slip in like a small fish between his ribs,
nudge the coral of his brain with my lips,
brushing over the blue coils of his bowels
with the fluted silk of my tail.
Death is not romantic. He is dying. That fact
is stark and one-dimensional, a black note
on an empty staff. My feet are cold,
but not as cold as his, and I hate this music
that floods the cramped insides
of my car, my head, slowing the world down
with its lurid majesty, transforming
everything I see into stained memorials
to life—even the old Ford ahead of me,
its battered rear end thinned to scallops of rust,
pumping grim shrouds of exhaust
into the shimmering air—even the tenacious
nasturtiums clinging to a fence, stem and bloom
of the insignificant, music spooling
from their open faces, spilling upward, past
the last rim of blue and into the black pool
of another galaxy. As if all that emptiness
were a place of benevolence, a destination,
a peace we could rise to.

Family Stories

I had a boyfriend who told me stories about his family,
how an argument once ended when his father
seized a lit birthday cake in both hands
and hurled it out a second-story window. That,
I thought, was what a normal family was like: anger
sent out across the sill, landing like a gift
to decorate the sidewalk below. In mine
it was fists and direct hits to the solar plexus,
and nobody ever forgave anyone. But I believed
the people in his stories really loved one another,
even when they yelled and shoved their feet
through cabinet doors or held a chair like a bottle
of cheap champagne, christening the wall,
rungs exploding from their holes.
I said it sounded harmless, the pomp and fury
of the passionate. He said it was a curse
being born Italian and Catholic and when he
looked from that window what he saw was the moment
rudely crushed. But all I could see was a gorgeous
three-layer cake gliding like a battered ship
down the sidewalk, the smoking candles broken, sunk
deep in the icing, a few still burning.

Pearl

> She was a headlong assault, a hysterical discharge,
> an act of total extermination.
>
> —MYRA FRIEDMAN,
> *Buried Alive: The Biography of Janis Joplin*

She was nothing much, this plain-faced girl from Texas,
this moonfaced child who opened her mouth
to the gravel pit churning in her belly, acne-faced
daughter of Leadbelly, Bessie, Otis, and the booze-
filled moon, child of the honkytonk bar-talk crowd
who cackled like a bird of prey, velvet cape blown
open in the Monterey wind, ringed fingers fisted
at her throat, howling the slagheap up and out
into the sawdusted air. Barefaced, mouth warped
and wailing like giving birth, like being eaten alive
from the inside, or crooning like the first child
abandoned by God, trying to woo him back,
down on her knees and pleading for a second chance.
When she sang she danced a stand-in-place dance,
one foot stamping at that fire, that bed of coals;
one leg locked at the knee and quivering, the other
pumping its oil-rig rhythm, her boy hip jigging
so the beaded belt slapped her thigh.
Didn't she give it to us? So loud so hard so furious,
hurling heat-seeking balls of lightning
down the long human aisles, her voice crashing
into us—sonic booms to the heart—this little white girl
who showed us what it was like to die
for love, to jump right up and die for it night after
drumbeaten night, going down shrieking—hair
feathered, frayed, eyes glazed, addicted to the song—
a one-woman let me show you how it's done, how it is,

where it goes when you can't hold it in anymore.
Child of everything gone wrong, gone bad, gone down,
gone. Girl with the girlish breasts and woman hips,
thick-necked, sweat misting her upper lip, hooded eyes
raining a wild blue light, hands reaching out
to the ocean we made, all that anguish and longing
swelling and rising at her feet. Didn't she burn
herself up for us, shaking us alive? That child,
that girl, that rawboned woman, stranded
in a storm on a blackened stage like a house
on fire.

Smoke

Who would want to give it up, the coal
a cat's eye in the dark room, no one there
but you and your smoke, the window
cracked to street sounds, the distant cries
of living things. Alone, you are almost
safe, smoke slipping out between the sill
and the glass, sucked into the night
you don't dare enter, its eyes drunk
and swimming with stars. Somewhere
a dumpster is ratcheted open by the claws
of a black machine. All down the block
something inside you opens and shuts.
Sinister screech, pneumatic wheeze,
trash slams into the chute: leftovers, empties.
You don't flip on the TV or the radio, they
might muffle the sound of car engines
backfiring, and in the silence between,
streetlights twitching from green to red, scoff
of footsteps, the rasp of breath, your own,
growing lighter and lighter as you inhale.
There's no music for this scarf of smoke
wrapped around your shoulders, its fingers
crawling the pale stem of your neck,
no song light enough, liquid enough,
that climbs high enough before it thins
and disappears. Death's shovel scrapes
the sidewalk, critches across the man-made
cracks, slides on grease into rain-filled gutters,
digs its beveled nose among the ravaged leaves.
You can hear him weaving his way
down the street, sloshed on the last breath
he swirled past his teeth before swallowing:

breath of the cat kicked to the curb, a woman's
sharp grasp, lung-filled wail of the shaken child.
You can't put it out, can't stamp out the light
and let the night enter you, let it burrow through
your smallest passages. So you listen and listen
and smoke and give thanks, suck deep
with the grace of the living, blowing halos
and nooses and zeros and rings, the blue chains
linking around your head. Then you pull it in
again, the vein-colored smoke,
and blow it up toward a ceiling you can't see
where it lingers like a sweetness you can never hold,
like the ghost the night will become.

The Orgasms of Organisms

Above the lawn the wild beetles mate
and mate, skew their tough wings
and join. They light in our hair,
on our arms, fall twirling and twinning
into our laps. And below us, in the grass,
the bugs are seeking each other out,
antennae lifted and trembling, tiny legs
scuttling, then the infinitesimal
ahs of their meeting, the awkward joy
of their turnings around. O end to end
they meet again and swoon as only bugs can.
This is why, sometimes, the grass feels electric
under our feet, each blade quivering, and why
the air comes undone over our heads
and washes down around our ears like rain.
But it has to be spring, and you have to be
in love—acutely, painfully, achingly in love—
to hear the black-robed choir of their sighs.

and remote, and useful,
if only to itself. Take the fly, angel
of the ordinary house, laying its bright
eggs on the trash, pressing each jewel out
delicately along a crust of buttered toast.
Bagged, the whole mess travels to the nearest
dump where other flies have gathered, singing
over stained newsprint and reeking
fruit. Rapt on air they execute an intricate
ballet above the clashing pirouettes
of heavy machinery. They hum with life.
While inside rumpled sacks pure white
maggots writhe and spiral from a rip,
a tear-shaped hole that drools and drips
a living froth onto the buried earth.
The warm days pass, gulls scree and pitch,
rats manage the crevices, feral cats abandon
their litters for a morsel of torn fur, stranded
dogs roam open fields, sniff the fragrant edges,
a tossed lacework of bones and shredded flesh.
And the maggots tumble at the center, ripening,
husks membrane-thin, embryos darkening
and shifting within, wings curled and wet,
the open air pungent and ready to receive them
in their fecund iridescence. And so, of our homely hosts,
a bag of jewels is born again into the world. Come, lost
children of the sun-drenched kitchen, your parents
soundly sleep along the windowsill, content,
wings at rest, nestled in against the warm glass.
Everywhere the good life oozes from the useless
waste we make when we create—our streets teem
with human young, rafts of pigeons streaming

over the squirrel-burdened trees. If there is
a purpose, maybe there are too many of us
to see it, though we can, from a distance,
hear the dull thrum of generation's industry,
feel its fleshly wheel churn the fire inside us, pushing
the world forward toward its ragged edge, rushing
like a swollen river into multitude and rank disorder.
Such abundance. We are gorged, engorging, and gorgeous.

from

FACTS

ABOUT

THE

MOON

Facts About the Moon

The moon is backing away from us
an inch and a half each year. That means
if you're like me and were born
around fifty years ago the moon
was a full six feet closer to the earth.
What's a person supposed to do?
I feel the gray cloud of consternation
travel across my face. I begin thinking
about the moon-lit past, how if you go back
far enough you can imagine the breathtaking
hugeness of the moon, prehistoric
solar eclipses when the moon covered the sun
so completely there was no corona, only
a darkness we had no word for.
And future eclipses will look like this: the moon
a small black pupil in the eye of the sun.
But these are bald facts.
What bothers me most is that someday
the moon will spiral right out of orbit
and all land-based life will die.
The moon keeps the oceans from swallowing
the shores, keeps the electromagnetic fields
in check at the polar ends of the earth.
And please don't tell me
what I already know, that it won't happen
for a long time. I don't care. I'm afraid
of what will happen to the moon.
Forget us. We don't deserve the moon.
Maybe we once did but not now
after all we've done. These nights
I harbor a secret pity for the moon, rolling
around alone in space without

Moon in the Window

I wish I could say I was the kind of child
who watched the moon from her window,
would turn toward it and wonder.
I never wondered. I read. Dark signs
that crawled toward the edge of the page.
It took me years to grow a heart
from paper and glue. All I had
was a flashlight, bright as the moon,
a white hole blazing beneath the sheets.

her milky planet, her only love, a mother
who's lost a child, a bad child,
a greedy child or maybe a grown boy
who's murdered and raped, a mother
can't help it, she loves that boy
anyway, and in spite of herself
she misses him, and if you sit beside her
on the padded hospital bench
outside the door to his room you can't not
take her hand, listen to her while she
weeps, telling you how sweet he was,
how blue his eyes, and you know she's only
romanticizing, that she's conveniently
forgotten the bruises and booze,
the stolen car, the day he ripped
the phones from the walls, and you want
to slap her back to sanity, remind her
of the truth: he was a leech, a fuckup,
a little shit, and you almost do
until she lifts her pale puffy face, her eyes
two craters, and then you can't help it
either, you know love when you see it,
you can feel its lunar strength, its brutal pull.

The Crossing

The elk of Orick wait patiently to cross the road
and my husband of six months, who thinks

he's St. Francis, climbs out of the car to assist.
Ghost of St. Francis, his T-shirt flapping, steps

tenderly onto the tarmac and they begin their trek,
heads lifted, nostrils flared, each footfall

a testament to stalled momentum, gracefully
hesitant, as a brace of semis, lined up, humming,

adjust their air brakes. They cross the four-lane
like a coronation, slow as a Greek frieze, river

wind riffling the wheat grass of their rumps.
But my husband stays on, to talk to the one

who won't budge, oblivious to her sisters,
a long stalk of fennel gyrating between her teeth.

Go on, he beseeches, *Get going,* but the lone elk
stands her ground, their noses less than a yard apart.

One stubborn creature staring down another.
This is how I know the marriage will last.

The Ravens of Denali

Such dumb luck. To stumble
across an "unkindness" of ravens
at play with a shred of clear visquine
fallen from the blown-out window
of the Denali Truck Stop and Café.
Black wings gathering in the deserted
parking lot below the Assembly of God.
Ravens at play in the desolate fields
of the lord, under the tallest mountain
in North America, eight of them,
as many as the stars in the Big Dipper
on Alaska's state flag, yellow stars
sewn to a blue background flapping
from a pole over the roadside.
Flag that Benny Benson, age 13,
an Alutiiq Indian of Seward
formerly housed at the Jesse-Lee Memorial
Home for Orphans in Unalaska,
designed and submitted to a contest
in 1927 and won, his crayoned masterpiece
snapping above every broken-down
courthouse, chipped brick library
and deathtrap post office
in the penultimate state accepted
to the Union, known to its people
as the Upper One. Though a design
of the northern lights would have been
my choice, those alien green curtains
swirling over Mt. McKinley, Denali,
"the tall one," during the coldest, darkest
months of the subarctic year.
Red starburst or purple-edged skirt

rolling in vitreous waves
over the stunted ice-rimed treetops
or in spring, candles of fireweed
and the tiny ice blue flowers
of the tundra. Tundra, a word
that sounds like a thousand caribou
pouring down a gorge.
But all that might be difficult
for an orphaned 7th grader to draw
with three chewed-up crayons
and a piece of butcher paper.
As would these eight giggling ravens
with their shrewd eyes and slit-shine wings,
beaks like keloid scars. Acrobats
of speed and sheen. Black boot
of the bird family. Unconcerned
this moment with survival.
Though I hope they survive.
Whatever we have in store for them.
And the grizzly bear and the club-
footed moose. The muscular salmon.
The oil-spill seal and gull.
And raven's cousin, the bald eagle,
who can dive at 100 miles per hour,
can actually swim with massive
butterfly strokes through
the great glacial lakes of Alaska,
her wingspan as long as a man.
Architect of the two-ton nest
assembled over 34 years
with scavenged branches,
threatened in all but three
of the Lower 48, but making, by god,
a comeback if it's not too late
for such lofty promises.

Even the homely marmot
and the immigrant starling,
I wish you luck,
whatever ultimate harm we do
to this northernmost up-flung arm
of our country, our revolving world.
But you, epicurean raven, may you
be the pole star of the apocalypse,
you stubborn snow-trudger,
you quorum of eight who jostle one another
for a strip of plastic on the last
endless day, the last endless night
of our only sun's solar wind,
those glorious auroras, glassine gowns
of Blake's angels, that almost invisible shine
tugged and stretched between you
like taffy from outer space, tattered ends
gripped in your fur-crested beaks as we reel
headlong into the dwindling unknown.
Denizens of the frozen north, the last
frontier, harbingers of unluck
and the cold bleak lack to come.

The Life of Trees

The pines rub their great noise
into the spangled dark, scratch
their itchy boughs against the house,
and that moan's mystery translates roughly
into drudgery of ownership: time
to drag the ladder from the shed,
climb onto the roof with a saw
between my teeth, cut
those suckers down. What's reality
if not a long exhaustive cringe
from the blade, the teeth? I want to sleep
and dream the life of trees, beings
from the muted world who care
nothing for Money, Politics, Power,
Will or Right, who want little from the night
but a few dead stars going dim, a white owl
lifting from their limbs, who want only
to sink their roots into the wet ground
and terrify the worms or shake
their bleary heads like fashion models
or old hippies. If trees could speak
they wouldn't, only hum some low
green note, roll their pinecones
down the empty streets and blame it,
with a shrug, on the cold wind.
During the day they sleep inside
their furry bark, clouds shredding
like ancient lace above their crowns.
Sun. Rain. Snow. Wind. They fear
nothing but the Hurricane, and Fire,
that whipped bully who rises up
and becomes his own dead father.

In the storms the young ones
bend and bend and the old know
they may not make it, go down
with the power lines sparking,
broken at the trunk. They fling
their branches, forked sacrifice
to the beaten earth. They do not pray.
If they make a sound it's eaten
by the wind. And though the stars
return they do not offer thanks, only
ooze a sticky sap from their roundish
concentric wounds, clap the water
from their needles, straighten their spines
and breathe, and breathe again.

What's Broken

The slate black sky. The middle step
of the back porch. And long ago

my mother's necklace, the beads
rolling north and south. Broken

the rose stem, water into drops, glass
knob on the bedroom door. Last summer's

pot of parsley and mint, white roots
shooting like streamers through the cracks.

Years ago the cat's tail, the bird bath,
the car hood's rusted latch. Broken

little finger on my right hand at birth—
I was pulled out too fast. What hasn't

been rent, divided, split? Broken
the days into nights, the night sky

into stars, the stars into patterns
I make up as I trace them

with a broken-off blade
of grass. Possible, unthinkable,

the cricket's tiny back as I lie
on the lawn in the dark, my heart

a blue cup fallen from someone's hands.

Afterlife

Even in heaven, when a former waitress goes out
for lunch, she can't help it, can't stop wiping down
the counter, brushing crumbs from the bottoms
of ketchup bottles, cleaning the chunky rim
around the cap with a napkin, tipping big.
Old habits die hard. Old waitresses
die harder, laid out in cheap cardboard coffins
in their lacy blue varicose veins, arches fallen
like grand cathedrals, a row of female Quasimodos:
each finely sprung spine humped from a lifetime
hefting trays. But they have smiles on their faces,
feet up, dancing shoes shined, wispy hair nets
peeled off and tossed in the trash, permed strands
snagged in the knots. You hover over their open caskets
with your fist full of roses and it's their hands
you can't stop staring at. Hands like yours, fingers
scarred, stained, rough, muscles plump
between each knuckle, tough as a man's,
useless now, still as they never were
even at shift's end, gnarled wings folded
between the breasts of faceless women done
with their gossip, their earthly orders,
having poured the day's dark brew
into the last bottomless cup, finished
with mice in the rice bags, roaches
in the walk-in, their eyes sealed shut, deaf
forever to the clatter, the cook, the cries
of the living. Grateful as nuns. Quite dead.

Savages

for Matthew, Mike, Michael and Carl

They buy poetry like gang members
buy guns—for aperture, caliber,
heft and defense. They sit on the floor
in the stacks, thumbing through Keats
and Plath, Levine and Olds, four boys
in a bookstore, black glasses, brackish hair,
rumpled shirts from the bin at St. Vincent de Paul.
One slides a warped hardback
from the bottom shelf, the others
scoot over to check the dates,
the yellowed sheaves ride smooth
under their fingers.
One reads a stanza in a whisper,
another turns the page, and their heads
almost touch, temple to temple—toughs
in a huddle, barbarians before a hunt, kids
hiding in an alley while sirens spiral by.
When they finish reading one closes
the musty cover like the door
on Tutankhamen's tomb. They are savage
for knowledge, for beauty and truth.
They crawl on their knees to find it.

Vacation Sex

We've been at it all summer, from the Canadian border
to the edge of Mexico, just barely keeping it American
but doing okay just the same, in hotels under overpasses
or rooms next to ice machines, friends' fold-out couches,
in-laws' guest quarters—wallpaper and bedspreads festooned
with nautical rigging, tiny life rings and coiled tow ropes—

even one night in the car, the plush backseat not plush
enough, the door handle giving me an impromptu
sacro-cranial chiropractic adjustment, the underside
of the front seat strafing the perfect arches of his feet.
And one long glorious night in a cabin tucked in the woods
where our crooning and whooping started the coyotes

singing. But the best was when we got home, our luggage
cuddled in the vestibule—really just a hallway
but because we were home it seemed like a vestibule—
and we threw off our vestments, which were really
just our clothes but they seemed like garments, like raiment,
like habits because we felt sorely religious, dropping them

one by one on the stairs: white shirts, black bra, blue jeans,
red socks, then stood naked in our own bedroom, our bed
with its drab spread, our pillows that smelled like us:
a little shampoo-y, maybe a little like myrrh, the gooseberry
candle we light sometimes when we're in the mood for mood,
our own music and books and cap off the toothpaste and cat

on the window seat. Our window looks over a parking lot—
a dental group—and at night we can hear the cars whisper past
the 24-hour Albertson's where the homeless couple

buys their bag of wine before they walk across the street
to sit on the dentist's bench under a tree and swap it
and guzzle it and argue loudly until we all fall asleep.

Democracy

When you're cold—November, the streets icy and everyone you pass
homeless, Goodwill coats and Hefty bags torn up to make ponchos—
someone is always at the pay phone, hunched over the receiver

spewing winter's germs, swollen lipped, face chapped, making the last
tired connection of the day. You keep walking to keep the cold
at bay, too cold to wait for the bus, too depressing the thought

of entering that blue light, the chilled eyes watching you decide
which seat to take: the man with one leg, his crutches bumping
the smudged window glass, the woman with her purse clutched

to her breasts like a dead child, the boy, pimpled, morose, his head
shorn, a swastika carved into the stubble, staring you down.
So you walk into the cold you know: the wind, indifferent blade,

familiar, the gold leaves heaped along the gutters. You have
a home, a house with gas heat, a toilet that flushes. You have
a credit card, cash. You could take a taxi if one would show up.

You can feel it now: why people become Republicans: *Get that dog
off the street. Remove that spit and graffiti. Arrest those people huddled
on the steps of the church.* If it weren't for them you could believe in god,

in freedom, the bus would appear and open its doors, the driver dressed
in his tan uniform, pants legs creased, dapper hat: *Hello Miss, watch
your step now.* But you're not a Republican. You're only tired, hungry,

you want out of the cold. So you give up, step into line behind
the grubby vet who hides a bag of wine under his pea coat, holds out
his grimy 85 cents, takes each step slow as he pleases, releases his coins

into the box and waits as they chink down the chute, stakes out a seat
in the back and eases his body into the stained vinyl to dream
as the chips of shrapnel in his knee warm up and his good leg

flops into the aisle. And you'll doze off, too, in a while, next to the girl
who can't sit still, who listens to her Walkman and taps her boots
to a rhythm you can't hear, but you can see it—when she bops

her head and her hands do a jive in the air—you can feel it
as the bus rolls on, stopping at each red light in a long wheeze,
jerking and idling, rumbling up and lurching off again.

Face Poem

Your craggy mountain goat face.
Your mole-ridden, whiskered, stumpy fish of a face. Face
I turn to, face I trust, face I trace with grateful fingertips,
jaw like a hinge, washboard forehead, the deep scar a gnarl
along the scritch of your chin.
Your steep, crumbling cliff of a face.
Your U-Haul, bulldozer, crane of a face. Face worthy
of a thousand-dollar bill, a thickly poured, stamped, minted
and excavated coin. Your mile-high billboard of a face looming
up from the pillow of sighs.
Your used car lot of a face, the bumpers
and sprung hoods and headlights of your eyes, your DieHard
battery of a face, the pulpy pith of it, the flare and slur and flange
of your ears, the subterranean up-thrust ridge of your nose.
Your many-planed, light-catching, shadow-etched face.
Your sallow, sun-wracked, jowl-hung face. Eye flash
in flesh folds, gunnel rope and upper lip storm on the high seas
thrash of a face. Your been-there, done-that, anything-goes face.
Luck-of-the-draw fabulous four clubs five-knuckled slug
of a face. Toss of the dice face.

Superglue

I'd forgotten how fast it happens, the blush of fear
and the feeling of helpless infantile stupidity, stooped
over the sink, warm water gushing into a soapy bowl,
my stuck fingers plunged in, knuckles bumping the glass
like a stillborn pig in formaldehyde, my aging eyes
straining to read the warning label in minus two type,
lifting the dripping deformed thing up every few seconds
to stare, unbelieving, at the seamless joining, the skin
truly bonded as they say happens *immediately*, thinking:
Truth in Labeling, thinking: This is how I began inside
my mother's belly, before I divided toe from toe, bloomed
into separation like a peach-colored rose, my eyes going slick
and opening, my mouth releasing itself from itself to make
lips, legs one thick fin of trashing flesh wanting to be two,
unlocking from ankles to knees, cells releasing between
my thighs, not stopping there but wanting more double-ness,
up to the crotch and into the crotch, needing the split
to go deeper, carve a core, a pit, a two-sided womb, with
or without me my body would perform this sideshow
trick and then like a crack in a sidewalk
stop. And I'd carry that want for the rest of my life,
eyes peeled open, mouth agape, the world
piled around me with its visible seams: cheap curtains,
cupboard doors, cut bread on a plate, my husband
appearing in the kitchen on his two strong legs
to see what's wrong, lifting my hand by the wrist.
And I want to kiss him, to climb him,
to stuff him inside me and fill that space, poised
on the brink of opening opening opening
as my wrinkled fingers, pale and slippery,
remember themselves, and part.

Cello

When a dead tree falls in a forest
it often falls into the arms
of a living tree. The dead,
thus embraced, rasp in wind,
slowly carving a niche
in the living branch, shearing away
the rough outer flesh, revealing
the pinkish, yellowish, feverish
inner bark. For years
the dead tree rubs its fallen body
against the living, building
its dead music, making its raw mark,
wearing the tough bough down
as it moans and bends, the deep
rosined bow sound of the living
shouldering the dead.

Little Magnolia

Not nearly a woman like the backyard cedar
whose branches fall and curl,
whose curved body sways in wind,
the little magnolia is still a girl,
her first blossoms tied like white strips of rag
to the tips of her twiggy pigtails.

Who are the trees? They live
half in air, half below ground,

both rooted and homeless, like the man
who wedges his life between
the windbreak wall of the Laundromat
and the broken fence, a strip of gritty earth
where he's unfolded his section
of clean cardboard, his Goodwill blanket.
Here's his cup, his candle, his knife.

Starling

Tail a fanfare and the devil's
kindling. Oh to be a rider
on that purple storm. Not
peacock or eagle but lowly
starling, Satan's bird,
spreading her spotted wings
over the Valley of Bones.
To build a home within her, stark
shanty for the soul, bonfire stoked
with pine-sap sage, smoke
rising through her ribs, her skin,
tainting the undersides of leaves.
Marrow house from which the one
wild word escapes. Stave and barrel
world of want. Of late, my plush
black nest. My silver claw
and gravel craw. My only song.

from

THE BOOK
OF MEN

Staff Sgt. Metz

Metz is alive for now, standing in line
at the airport Starbucks in his camo gear
and buzz cut, his beautiful new
camel-colored suede boots. His hands
are thick-veined. The good blood
still flows through, given an extra surge
when he slurps his latte, a fleck of foam
caught on his bottom lip.

I can see into the canal in his right ear,
a narrow darkness spiraling deep inside his head
toward the place of dreaming and fractions,
ponds of quiet thought.

In the sixties my brother left for Vietnam,
a war no one understood, and I hated him for it.
When my boyfriend was drafted I made a vow
to write a letter every day, and then broke it.
I was a girl torn between love and the idea of love.
I burned their letters in the metal trash bin
behind the broken fence. It was the summer of love
and I wore nothing under my cotton vest,
my Mexican skirt.

I see Metz later, outside baggage claim,
hunched over a cigarette, mumbling
into his cell phone. He's more real to me now
than my brother was to me then, his big eyes
darting from car to car as they pass.
I watch him breathe into his hands.

I don't believe in anything anymore:
god, country, money or love.

All that matters to me now
is his life, the body so perfectly made,
mysterious in its workings, its oiled
and moving parts, the whole of him
standing up and raising one arm
to hail a bus, his legs pulling him forward,
all muscle and sinew and living gristle,
the countless bones of his foot trapped in his boot,
stepping off the red curb.

Bakersfield, 1969

I used to visit a boy in Bakersfield, hitchhike
to the San Diego terminal and ride the bus for hours
through the sun-blasted San Fernando Valley
just to sit on his fold-down bed in a trailer
parked in the side yard of his parents' house,
drinking Southern Comfort from a plastic cup.
His brother was a sessions man for Taj Mahal,
and he played guitar, too, picked at it like a scab.
Once his mother knocked on the tin door
to ask us in for dinner. She watched me
from the sides of her eyes while I ate.
When I offered to wash the dishes she told me
she wouldn't stand her son being taken
advantage of. I said I had no intention
of taking anything and set the last dish
carefully in the rack. He was a bit slow,
like he'd been hit hard on the back of the head,
but nothing dramatic. We didn't talk much anyway,
just drank and smoked and fucked and slept
through the ferocious heat. I found a photograph
he took of me getting back on the bus or maybe
stepping off into his arms. I'm wearing jeans
with studs punched into the cuffs,
a T-shirt with stars on the sleeves, a pair
of stolen bowling shoes and a purse I made
while I was in the loony bin, wobbly X's
embroidered on burlap with gaudy orange yarn.
I don't remember how we met. When I look
at this picture I think I might not even
remember this boy if he hadn't taken it
and given it to me, written his name under mine
on the back. I stopped seeing him

after that thing with his mother. I didn't know
I didn't know anything yet. I liked him.
That's what I remember. That,
and the I-don't-know-what degree heat
that rubbed up against the trailer's metal sides,
steamed in through the cracks between the door
and porthole windows, pressed down on us
from the ceiling and seeped through the floor,
crushing us into the damp sheets. How we endured it,
sweat streaming down our naked bodies, the air
sucked from our lungs as we slept. Taj Mahal says
If you ain't scared, you ain't right. Back then
I was scared most of the time. But I acted
tough, like I knew every street.
What I liked about him was that he wasn't acting.
Even his sweat tasted sweet.

Juneau Spring

In Alaska I slept in a bed on stilts, one arm
pressed against the ice-feathered window,
the heat on high, sweat darkening the collar
of my cotton thermals. I worked hard to buy that bed,
hiked toward it when the men in the booths
were finished crushing hundred-dollar bills
into my hand, pitchers of beer balanced on my shoulder
set down like pots of gold. My shift ended at 5 AM:
station tables wiped clean, salt and peppers
replenished, ketchups married. I walked the dirt road
in my stained apron and snow boots, wool scarf,
second-hand gloves, steam rising
off the backs of horses wading chest deep in fog.
I walked home slow under Orion, his starry belt
heavy beneath the cold carved moon.
My room was still, quiet, squares of starlight
set down like blank pages on the yellow quilt.
I left the heat on because I could afford it, the house
hot as a sauna, and shed my sweater and skirt,
toed off my boots, slung my damp socks
over the oil heater's coils. I don't know now
why I ever left. I slept like the dead
while outside my window the sun rose
low over the glacier, and the glacier did its best
to hold on, though one morning I woke to hear it
giving up, sloughing off a chunk of antediluvian ice,
a sound like an iron door opening on a bent hinge.
Those undefined days I stared into the blue scar
where the ice face had been, so clear and crystalline
it hurt. I slept in my small room and all night—
or what passed for night that far north—

the geography of the world outside my window
was breaking and falling and changing shape.
And I woke to it and looked at it and didn't speak.

Mine Own Phil Levine

after W. S. Merwin

What he told me, I will tell you
There was a war on
It seemed we had lived through
Too many to name, to number

There was no arrogance about him
No vanity, only the strong backs
Of his words pressed against
The tonnage of a page

His suggestion to me was that hard work
Was the order of each day
When I asked again, he said it again,
Pointing it out twice

His Muse, if he had one, was a window
Filled with a brick wall, the left hand corner
Of his mind, a hand lined with grease
And sweat: literal things

Before I knew him, I was unknown
I drank deeply from his knowledge
A cup he gave me again and again
Filled with water, clear river water

He was never old, and never grew older
Though the days passed and the poems
Marched forth and they were his words
Only, no other words were needed

He advised me to wait, to hold true
To my vision, to speak in my own voice
To say the thing straight out
There was the whole day about him

The greatest thing, he said, was presence
To be yourself in your own time, to stand up
That poetry was precision, raw precision
Truth and compassion: genius

I had hardly begun. I asked, How did you begin
He said, I began in a tree, in Lucerne
In a machine shop, in an open field
Start anywhere

He said If you don't write, it won't
Get written. No tricks. No magic
About it. He gave me his gold pen
He said What's mine is yours

Late-Night TV

Again the insomnia of August,
a night sky buffed by the heat,
the air so still a ringing phone
three blocks away sings
through the fan's slow moving blades.
The sleeping cat at the foot of the bed
twitches in a pool of dusty sheets,
her fur malt-colored, electric.

Time to rub the shoulder's tight knots out
with a thumb, flip on the TV, watch a man
douse a white blouse with ink before dipping
that sad sleeve into a clear bucket.

What cup of love poured him into this world?
Did his mother touch her lips
to his womb-battered crown
and inhale his scent?
Did his new father lift him and name him?
He was fed, clothed, taught to talk.
Someone must have picked him up
each time he wobbled and fell.
There might have been a desk, a history book,
pencils in a box, a succession
of wheeled toys.

By what back road did he travel
to this late-night station?
By what untraceable set of circumstances
did he arrive in my bedroom on a summer night,
pinching a shirt collar between his fingers,
his own invention locked in a blue box,
a rainbow slashed across it?

Somewhere in the universe is a palace
where each of us is imprinted with a map,
the one path seared into the circuits of our brains.
It signals us to turn left at the green light,
right at the dead tree.

We know nothing about how it all works,
how we end up in one bed or another,
speak one language instead of the others,
what heat draws us to our life's work
or keeps us from a dream until it's nothing
but a blister we scratch in our sleep.

His voice is soothing, his teeth crooked,
his arms strong and smooth below rolled-up cuffs.
I have the power to make him disappear
with one touch, though if I do the darkness
will swallow me, drown me.

Time to settle back against the pillows,
gaze deeply into the excitement
welling in his eyes. It's a miracle, he whispers
as the burnt moon slips across the sky,
then he dumps the grainy crystals in
and stirs the water with a wooden spoon.

Smell of diesel fuel and dead trees
on a flatbed soaked to the bone.
Smell of dusty heater coils.
We got homicides in motels and apartments
all across the city: under the beds,
behind the doors, in the bathtubs.
It's where I come in at 5 AM,
paper cup of coffee dripping
down my sleeve, powdered
half-moon donut in my mouth.
Blood everywhere. Bodies
belly down, bodies faceup
on the kitchenette floor.
¿Dónde está? Que será.
We got loose ends, we got
dead ends, we got split ends,
hair in the drains, fingerprints
on glass. This is where I stand,
my hat glittery with rain,
casting my restless shadow.

These are the dark hours,
dark times are these, hours
when the clock chimes once
as if done with it, tired of it: the sun,
the highways, the damnable
flowers strewn on the fake wool rug.

These are the flayed heart's flowers,
oil-black dahlias big as fists,
stems thick as wrists, striped, torn,
floating in the syrupy left-on music

but the bright world is done and I'm
a ghost touching the hair of the dead
with a gloved hand.

These are the done-for, the poor,
the defenseless, mostly women,
felled trees, limbs lashing
up into air, into rain,
as if time were nothing, hours,
clocks, highways, faces, don't step
on the petals, the upturned hands, stay
behind the yellow tape, let
the photographer's hooded camera pass,
the coroner in his lab coat, the DA
in her creased black pants.

Who thought
to bring these distracting flowers?
Who pushed
out the screen and broke the lock?
Who let him in?
Who cut the phone cord, the throat,
the wrist, the cake
on a plate and sat down and ate
only half?

What good is my life if I can't read the clues,
my mind the glue and each puzzle piece
chewed by the long-gone dog who raced
through the door, ran through our legs
and knocked over the vase,
hurtled down the alley and into the street?

What are we but meat, flesh
and the billion veins to be bled?

Why do we die this way, our jaws
open, our eyes bulging, as if there
were something to see or say?
Though today the flowers speak to me,
the way they sprawl in the streaked light,
their velvet lips and lids opening as I watch,
as if they wanted to go on living, climb
my pant legs, my wrinkled shirt, reach up
past my throat and curl over my mouth,
my eyes. Bury me in bloom.

Mick Jagger (World Tour, 2008)

He stands on stage
after spot-lit stage, yowling
with his rubber mouth. If you
turn off the sound he's
a ruminating bovine,
a baby's face tasting his first
sour orange or spitting
spooned oatmeal out.
Rugose cheeks and beef
jerky jowls, shrubby hair
waxed, roughed up, arms
slung dome-ward, twisted
branches of a tough tree, knees
stomped high as his sunken chest.
Oddities aside, he's a hybrid
of stamina and slouch,
tummy pooch, pouches under
his famous invasive rolling eyes.
He flutters like the pages
of a dirty book, doing
the sombrero dance, rocking
the microphone's
round black foot, one hand
gripping the skinny metal rod,
the other pumping its victory fist
like he's flushing a chain toilet.
Old as the moon and sleek
as a puma circling the herd.
The vein on his forehead
pops. His hands drop into fists.
He bows like a beggar then rises
like a monarch. Sir Mick,

our bony ruler. Jagger, slumping
off stage shining with sweat.
Oh please don't die, not now,
not ever, not yet.

Men

It's tough being a guy, having to be gruff
and buff, the strong silent type, having to laugh
it off—pain, loss, sorrow, betrayal—or leave in a huff
and say *No big deal*, take a ride, listen to enough
loud rock and roll that it scours out your head, if
not your heart. Or to be called a fag or a poof
when you love something or someone, scuffing
a shoe across the floor, hiding a smile in a muffler
pulled up nose high, an eyebrow raised for the word quaff
used in casual conversation—wine, air, oil change at the Jiffy
Lube—gulping it down, a joke no one gets. It's rough,
yes, the tie around the neck, the starched white cuffs
too long, too short, frayed, frilled, rolled up. The self
isn't an easy quest for a beast with balls, a cock, proof
of something difficult to define or defend. Chief or chef,
thief or roofer, serf or sheriff, feet on the earth or aloof.
Son, brother, husband, lover, father, they are different
from us, except when they fall or stand alone on a wharf.

Antilamentation

Regret nothing. Not the cruel novels you read
to the end just to find out who killed the cook, not
the insipid movies that made you cry in the dark,
in spite of your intelligence, your sophistication, not
the lover you left quivering in a hotel parking lot,
the one you beat to the punch line, the door or the one
who left you in your red dress and shoes, the ones
that crimped your toes, don't regret those.
Not the nights you called god names and cursed
your mother, sunk like a dog in the living room couch,
chewing your nails and crushed by loneliness.
You were meant to inhale those smoky nights
over a bottle of flat beer, to sweep stuck onion rings
across the dirty restaurant floor, to wear the frayed
coat with its loose buttons, its pockets full of struck matches.
You've walked those streets a thousand times and still
you end up here. Regret none of it, not one
of the wasted days you wanted to know nothing,
when the lights from the carnival rides
were the only stars you believed in, loving them
for their uselessness, not wanting to be saved.
You've traveled this far on the back of every mistake,
ridden in dark-eyed and morose but calm as a house
after the TV set has been pitched out the window.
Harmless as a broken ax. Emptied of expectation.
Relax. Don't bother remembering any of it. Let's stop here,
under the lit sign on the corner, and watch all the people walk by.

Cher

I wanted to be Cher, tall
as a glass of iced tea,
her bony shoulders draped
with a curtain of dark hair
that plunged straight down,
the cut tips brushing
her nonexistent butt.
I wanted to wear a lantern
for a hat, a cabbage, a piñata
and walk in thigh-high boots
with six-inch heels that buttoned
up the back. I wanted her
rouged cheek bones and her
throaty panache, her voice
of gravel and clover, the hokum
of her clothes: black fishnet
and pink pom-poms, frilled
halter tops, fringed bells
and her thin strip of waist
with the bullet-hole navel.
Cher standing with her skinny arm
slung around Sonny's thick neck,
posing in front of the Eiffel Tower,
The Leaning Tower of Pisa,
The Great Wall of China,
The Crumbling Pyramids, smiling
for the camera with her crooked
teeth, hit-and-miss beauty, the sun
bouncing off the bump on her nose.
Give me back the old Cher,
the gangly, imperfect girl
before the shaving knife

took her, before they shoved
pillows in her tits, injected
the lumpy gel into her lips.
Take me back to the woman
I wanted to be, stalwart
and silly, smart as her lion
tamer's whip, my body a torch
stretched the length of the polished
piano, legs bent at the knee, hair
cascading down over Sonny's blunt
fingers as he pummeled the keys,
singing in a sloppy alto
the oldest, saddest songs.

Dog Moon

The old dog next door won't stop barking
at the moon. My neighbor is keeping a log:
what time, how long, whether howling is involved.
I know she's awake as I am, robe askew,
calling animal control while I drink dark tea
and stare out my window at the voodoo moon,
throwing beads of light into the arms
of the bare-chested trees. Who can blame him
when the moon is as big as a kitchen clock
and ticking like a time bomb? The bright full moon
with its beryl core and striated face, its plasma umbra,
pouring borrowed light into every abyss on earth,
turning the rivers silver, plowing the mountains'
shadows across grasslands and deserts, towns
riddled with mineshafts, oil rigs and mills,
yellow tractors asleep in the untilled fields.
The what-were-they-like moon staring down
on rain-pocked gravestones, worming its way
into gopher holes, setting barbed wire fences ablaze.
Who wouldn't love this old-tooth moon,
this toilet-paper moon? This feral, flea-bitten moon
is that dog's moon, too. Certain-of-nothing moon, bone
he can't wait to sink his teeth into. Radio moon,
the white dial tuned to static. Panic moon,
pulling clouds like blankets over its baby face.
Moon a portrait hung from a nail
in the starred hallway of the past.
Full moon that won't last.
I can hear that dog clawing at the fence.
Moon a manhole cover sunk in the boulevard
of night, monocle on a chain, well of light,

a frozen pond lifted and thrown like a discus
onto the sky. I scratch my skull, look down
into my stained empty cup. That dog
has one blind eye, the other one's looking up.

Mother's Day

I passed through the narrow hills
of my mother's hips one cold morning
and never looked back, until now, clipping
her tough toenails, sitting on the bed's edge
combing out the tuft of hair at the crown
where it ratted up while she slept, her thumbs
locked into her fists, a gesture as old
as she is, her blanched knees fallen together
beneath a blue nightgown. The stroke

took whole pages of words, random years
torn from the calendar, the names of roses
leaning over her driveway: Cadenza,
Great Western, American Beauty. She can't
think, can't drink her morning tea, do her
crossword puzzle in ink. She's afraid
of everything, the sound of the front door
opening, light falling through the blinds—
pulls her legs up so the bright bars
won't touch her feet. I help her
with the buttons on her sweater. She looks
hard at me and says the word sleeve.
Exactly, I tell her and her face relaxes
for the first time in weeks. I lie down
next to her on the flowered sheets and tell her
a story about the day she was born, head
first into a hard world: the Great Depression,
shanties, Hoovervilles, railroads and unions.
I tell her about Amelia Earhart and she asks

Air? and points to the ceiling. Asks Heart?
and points to her chest. Yes, I say. I sing

Cole Porter songs, *Brother, Can You Spare
a Dime?* When I recite lines from *Gone
with the Wind* she sits up and says Potatoes!
and I say, Right again. I read her Sandburg,
some Frost, and she closes her eyes. I say yes,
yes, and tuck her in. It's summer. She's tired.
No one knows where she's been.

Dark Charms

Eventually the future shows up everywhere:
those burly summers and unslept nights in deep
lines and dark splotches, thinning skin.
Here's the corner store grown to a condo,
the bike reduced to one spinning wheel,
the ghost of a dog that used to be, her trail
no longer trodden, just a dip in the weeds.
The clear water we drank as thirsty children
still runs through our veins. Stars we saw then
we still see now, only fewer, dimmer, less often.
The old tunes play and continue to move us
in spite of our learning, the wraith of romance,
lost innocence, literature, the death of the poets.
We continue to speak, if only in whispers,
to something inside us that longs to be named.
We name it the past and drag it behind us,
bag like a lung filled with shadow and song,
dreams of running, the keys to lost names.

Lost in Costco

Our mother wandered the aisles in the city
of canned goods and 30-lb. sacks
of dog food, mountains of sweat pants
and cheap jeans, open bins of discounted CDs.
She rested for a moment on the edge
of a bed in the furniture section,
trying to remember if it was time to sleep,
then headed off to garden supplies
where she stared at the glazed pots, missing
her roses, the ones she planted
outside the house she had to sell with the tree
she wanted to be buried under, her ashes
sealed in a See's Candy tin. We found her
on a piano bench, her purse beside her
like a canvas familiar, her fingers
running over the keys, playing the songs
she loved, taking requests from the crowd
gathered under the buzzing fluorescent lights.
Faking it, picking out the tunes, striking
a chord like she'd do when we were young
and she'd say sing it to me and we'd hum
a few bars: pop songs and Top 40 hits,
TV theme songs or chewing gum jingles,
our high, sweet voices giving her
so little to go on.

Second Chances

What are the chances a raindrop
from last night's storm caught
in the upturned cup of an autumn leaf
will fall from this tree I pass under
and land on the tip of my lit cigarette,
snuffing it out? What are the chances
my niece will hit bottom before Christmas,
a drop we all long for, and quit heroin?
What are the chances of being hit
by a bus, a truck, a hell-bound train
or inheriting the gene for cancer,
addiction? What good are statistics
on a morning like this? What good
is my niece to anyone but herself?
What are the chances any of you
are reading this poem?
                              Dear men,
whom I have not met,
when you meet her on the street
wearing the wounds that won't heal
and she offers you the only thing
she has left, what are the chances
you'll take pity on her fallen body?

Fall

I'm tired of stories about the body,
how important it is, how unimportant,
how you're either a body
hauling a wrinkled brain around
or a brain trailing a stunned sheen
of flesh. Or those other questions
like Would you rather love or be loved?
If you could come back as the opposite sex,
what would you do first? As if. As if.
Yes the body is lonely, especially at twilight.
Yes Baptists would rather you not have a body at all,
especially not breasts, suspended in their hooked bras
like loose prayers, like ticking bombs, like two
Hallelujahs, the choir frozen in their onyx gowns
like a row of flashy Cadillacs, their plush upholstery
hidden behind tinted windows, Jesus swinging
from the rearview mirror by a chain.
And certainly not the body in the autumn
of its life, humming along in a wheelchair,
legs withered beneath the metallic shine
of thinning skin. No one wants to let
that body in. Especially not the breasts again.
Your mother's are strangers to you now, your sister's
were always bigger and clung to her blouse,
your lover's breasts, deep under the ground,
you weep beside the little mounds of earth
lightly shoveled over them.

Emily said she heard a fly buzz
when she died, heard it whizz
over her head, troubling her frizzed
hair. What will I hear? Showbiz
tunes on the radio, the megahertz
fuzz when the station picks up Yaz,
not the Hall-of-Famer or the Pez
of contraceptives, but the jazzy
flash-in-the-pan 80's techo-pop star, peach fuzz
on her rouged cheeks singing *Pul-ease*
Don't Go through a kazoo. Will my old love spritz
the air with the perfume of old roses,
buy me the white satin Mercedes-Benz
of pillows, string a rainbow blitz
of crystals in the window—quartz, topaz—
or will I die wheezing, listening to a quiz
show: What year is this? Who was the 44th Prez
of the United States? Where is the Suez
Canal? Are you too hot? Cold? Freezing.

The Secret of Backs

Heels of the shoes worn down, each
in its own way, sending signals to the spine.

The back of the knee as it folds and unfolds.
In winter the creases of American-made jeans:
blue denim seams worried to white thread.

And in summer, in spring, beneath the hems
of skirts, Bermudas, old bathing suit elastic,
the pleating and un-pleating of parchment skin.

And the dear, dear rears. Such variety! Such
choice in how to cover or reveal: belts looped high
or slung so low you can't help but think of plumbers.

And the small of the back: dimpled or taut, spiny or not,
tattooed, butterflied, rosed, winged, whorled. Maybe
still pink from the needle and ink. And shoulders,

broad or rolled, poking through braids, dreads, frothy
waterfalls of uncut hair, exposed to rain, snow, white
stars of dandruff, unbrushed flecks on a blue-black coat.

And the spiral near the top of the back of the head—
peek of scalp, exquisite galaxy—as if the first breach
had swirled each filament away from that startled center.

Ah, but the best are the bald or neatly shorn, revealing
the flanged, sun-flared, flamboyant backs of ears: secret
as the undersides of leaves, the flipside of flower petals.

And oh, the *oh my* nape of the neck. The up-swept *oh my*
nape of the neck. I could walk behind anyone and fall in love.

Don't stop. Don't turn around.

ONLY
AS THE DAY
IS LONG:
NEW
POEMS

Lapse

I am not deceived, I do not think it is still summer. I
see the leaves turning on their stems. I am
not oblivious to the sun as it lowers on its stem, not
fooled by the clock holding off, not deceived
by the weight of its tired hands holding forth. I
do not think my dead will return. They will not do
what I ask of them. Even if I plead on my knees. Not
even if I kiss their photographs or think
of them as I touch the things they left me. It
isn't possible to raise them from their beds, is
it? Even if I push the dirt away with my bare hands? Still-
ness, unearth their faces. Bring me the last dahlias of summer.

Before Surgery

In another life you might hear the song
of your neighbor clipping the hedges, a sound
oddly pleasant, three coarse dull snips,
three thin branches thumping softly as death
onto the closed doors of the mown lawn.

You might get your every dark wish: damson plums
for breakfast, mud swelling up between your toes
as you brush the green scum from the face of a pond
with a stick, gold carp flying like flocks of finches
through the azurite blue, a copperhead with a minnow
struggling in its mouth winding away from you.

In that hush you might hear the gods
mutter your name, diamonds of salt
melting on your tongue. You could lie there
molten and glowing as a blade hammered to silver
by the four-billion-year-old middle-aged sun.

In another life you might slip under canal after canal
in a coracle boat, look up to see river light
scribbling hieroglyphs on the curved undersides
of each stone arch. You might hear
an echo, the devil's fiddle
strummed just for you, and you might sing, too,
unbuckle your voice. You can't speak

the meaning of being. The nurses can't help you.
Beautiful as you are with your plasma eyes,
beautiful as they are in their mesh-blue protective booties,
their sugary-white dresses, so starched, so pressed.

Your deepest bones might ache with longing,
your skeleton draped in its finest flesh
like the lush velvet curtains that open slowly
before the opera begins.

Death of the Mother

> At the round earth's imagined corners, blow
> Your trumpets, angels, and arise, arise . . .
>
> —JOHN DONNE

At day's end: last sight, sound, smell and touch, blow
your final breath into the hospital's disinfected air, rise
from your bed, mother of eight, the blue scars of infinity
lacing your belly, your fractious hair and bony knees, and go
where we can never find you, where we can never overthrow
your lust for order, your love of chaos, your tyrannies
of despair, your can of beer. Cast down your nightshade eyes
and float through the quiet, your nightgown wrapped like woe
around your shredded soul, your cavernous heart, that space
you left us like a gift, brittle staircase of *ifs* we are bound
to climb too often and too late. Unleash us, let your grace
breathe over us in silence, when we can bear it, ground
as we are into our loss. You taught us how to glean the good
from anything, pardon anyone, even you, awash as we are in your blood.

Under Stars

When my mother died
I was as far away
as I could be, on an arm of land
floating in the Atlantic
where boys walk shirtless
down the avenue
holding hands, and gulls sleep
on the battered pilings,
their bright beaks hidden
beneath one white wing.

Maricopa, Arizona. Mea culpa.
I did not fly to see your body
and instead stepped out
on a balcony in my slip
to watch the stars turn
on their grinding wheel.
Early August, the ocean,
a salt-tinged breeze.

Botanists use the word
serotinous to describe
late-blossoming, *serotinal*
for the season of late summer.
I did not write your obituary
as my sister requested, could
not compose such final lines:
I closed the piano
to keep the music in. Instead

I stood with you
on what now seems

like the ancient deck
of a great ship, our nightgowns
flaring, the smell of dying lilacs
drifting up from someone's
untended yard, and we
listened to the stars hiss
into the bent horizon, blossoms
the sea gathered tenderly, each
shattered and singular one
long dead, but even so, incandescent,
making a singed sound, singing
as they went.

Changeable Weather

My mother might launch her thumb
into the air and say Get the hell
out of here or she might tell
us a parable about the quick and the dumb

pulling a splinter from a finger.
She'd linger at the back door
humming notes to a score
she was struggling to learn. Bring

me a cigarette she would shout

over her nightgowned shoulder.
The weather could change without
warning: clear morning, mountains
of cloud by noon. When you're older

she would snap, turning off the TV
or snatching a book from our hands,
then scuff across the rug, a phantom
in her blue robe and slippers. We

lost her daily, then found her, devout

over a bowl of cherries, turning
to spit the seeds over our upturned
faces, us flinching in unison when she hit
the wall, her red lips shaped in a kiss.

We never knew which way to run:
into her arms or away from her sharp eyes.
We loved her most when she was gone,
and when, after long absence, she arrived.

Only as the Day Is Long

Soon she will be no more than a passing thought,
a pang, a timpani of wind in the chimes, bent spoons
hung from the eaves on a first night in a new house
on a block where no dog sings, no cat visits
a neighbor cat in the middle of the street, winding
and rubbing fur against fur, throwing sparks.

Her atoms are out there, circling the earth, minus
her happiness, minus her grief, only her body's
water atoms, her hair and bone and teeth atoms,
her fleshy atoms, her boozy atoms, her saltines
and cheese and tea, but not her piano concerto
atoms, her atoms of laughter and cruelty, her atoms
of lies and lilies along the driveway and her slippers,
Lord her slippers, where are they now?

Think of the leaning note: a dissonance
    released by a consonance. Think
        of the crushed tone or tone clusters, notes

piling up around the legs of a piano bench
    like one-winged blackbirds,
        all eye and beak, fallen letters of the alphabet

spelling out what's missing. Think of purple bells
    of delphinium in a window box, their stained light,
        coarse granite slab chinked

into the semblance of a face, think of fate,
    how it embraces the ghost gowns of the past,
        the span of a hand, a clutch of keys,

a stick dragged along fence slats, the custom
    of taking off one's hat in church, scrap of lace
        draped over a child's still soft skull.

There are those for whom music is a staunch
    against an open wound, the piano a tomb
        into which the sparrows of sorrow tumble:

Clair de Lune perishes the terror of time,
    and rivers run through, scumbling up the rocks.
        Think of all that's left behind, whatever leaves

trails as it trembles: horse tail, fish fan, feathers, flutes,
    whispers like vespers in another room.
        We did not question the hours' rhythms,

the adagio of her hands, each a pale veined reckoning,
        the day gleaned of its moments, embroidered berries
                in the gathers of her dress, her scent unleashed

in a square of sun, one minute tilting into the next,
        our house a battered ship on which we tossed
                as she steered us through the afternoons.

My Mother's Colander

Holes in the shape of stars
punched in gray tin, dented,
cheap, beaten by each
of her children with a wooden spoon.

Noodle catcher, spaghetti stopper,
pouring cloudy rain into the sink,
swirling counter clockwise
down the drain, starch slime
on the backside, caught
in the piercings.

Scrubbed for sixty years, packed
and unpacked, the baby's
helmet during the cold war,
a sinking ship in the bathtub,
little boat of holes.

Dirt scooped in with a plastic
shovel, sifted to make cakes
and castles. Wrestled
from each other's hands,
its tin feet bent and re-bent.

Bowl daylight fell through
onto freckled faces, noon stars
on the pavement, the universe
we circled aiming jagged stones,
rung bells it caught and held.

We saved our money and sent away for it,
red plastic frame, clear plastic maze,
packaged sand siphoned into a slot, then freed
the ants into their new lives, little machines
of desire, watched them carry the white
bread crumbs late into the night
beneath a table lamp. Sweet dynasty.
We bent our queenly ten-year-old heads
over their busy industry in 1962, Uncle Milton's
personal note of thanks unfolded on the floor,
while underground the first nuclear warhead
was being released from the Polaris submarine,
and Christmas Island shook, shrouded in a fine
radioactive mist. And our mother sang
her apocalyptic gospel to anyone who'd listen,
the navy housing's gravel lots shimmering
with each sonic boom, began a savings account
for a fall-out shelter she said she knew we couldn't
possibly afford. The poor will die, she told us,
Who cares about us peasants? To them
we're only workers: dependable, expendable,
and then thrust her middle finger up
into the oniony kitchen air. The ants died
soon after, one by shriveled one, then in clumps;
they looked like spiders with all their legs
and antennae sticking crookedly out
from a pea-sized knot of ruined bodies.
She was reading *Fail Safe* between loads
of laundry and we were reading Uncle Milton's
cheerful instructions. Some questions have
no answers. That night we listened to the silence

occupy our room. We slept together in one bed,
heel to heel, head to head. We tunneled deep
beneath the covers and waited for the light.

The two young women in the house across the way
are singing old-world songs, ballads dredged up
from our muddy history, tragic myths of peril,
betrayal. Harmonies slip across the paint-flaked sills
of the open window like vapor, drift up
into the unfolding cones of the surrounding pines
where the scarlet tanager, flame of spring,
his blood-red body and jet-black wings, answers
with his territorial *chick-burr, chick-burr*, as the girls
trill through a series of Appalachian blue notes
and sliding tones, one strumming the African banjo,
the other plucking a classical viola.
They seem unreal, though I can see the fact
of them through the glass, their tumblers
of iced tea, their heads thrown back,
the sudden laughter. I like to think
they've always been this happy, though I know
they must have felt alone, the last of one
they love burning out like an ember, a distant star—
Barbara Allen, The Wayfaring Stranger—but I also know
they must have been visited by a miracle
like the doctor removing the bandage from my husband's
damaged eye, the new world rushing in.
Does the artist live to commemorate? Do the birds
long to sing? And how far have we traveled
to get here where a summer breeze unleashes
the scents of wild lavender and lily of the valley,
where every unmarked grave is covered with a carpet
of sweet alyssum, where the mother tanager sings
her softer song above the crowns of hemlock,
death bloom made poisonous when the blood

of Jesus seeped into its roots: Woomlick, Devil's
Flower and Gypsy Flower, Break-Your-Mother's-Heart.

My mother's idea of heaven was a pulse, nurses
in white spilling light across fields with hurricane
lamps, bandage rolls, syringes, pain killers,
stethoscopes, pressure cuffs, patella hammers.

Twice she almost died herself, and so knew heaven
was not the light moving toward her but the lights
over the operating table, those five blue spheres
a spaceship's landing gear hovering above

such alien beings as we are. My mother's idea
of heaven was a jar of peanut butter and saltine
crackers, a patient's chart and a pot of tea, notes
scribbled in her elegant hand: more *Morphine,*

Cortizone, Alprazolam. It was a quorum of doctors
in an elevator going up, blood swabbed from the walls,
the smell of bleach following her to the next bed,
the next crisis, the next head she would cradle like

a baby, rubbing gravel from a wound with a
green soap sponge. Plastic gloves, IV stands,
pocket light, Iris scissors, forceps, thermometer,
and her gold Caduceus emblem pin, its coiled snakes

and disembodied wings. Her shoes of breathable
white leather, stain-resistant, slip-resistant, padded
collars, 4-ply pillow-top insole, their signature blue hearts.
Her heaven was smoking Kents while feeding crows

in the parking lot, The God of Sleep, twenty minutes
of uninterrupted unconsciousness, an abyssal cot
in the break room next to a broken ventilator, flat
on her back, her split-shift night-shift back, her spine

with its bolts and bent crossbars, its stripped screws
and bony overgrowths, fusions and cages and allografts.
She was a shaft of light in the inner workings, her touch
a tincture, a gauze dressing, a salve, a room-temp

saline bath. She microwaved blankets
to slide over the dead so when the ones
who loved them filed in to say goodbye,
the body felt warm under their hands.

Crow

When the air conditioner comes on it sounds for all the world
like my mother clearing her throat, and then sighing.

After she died I'd shudder and look up
expecting to see her ghost. I wasn't afraid, only hopeful.

To see her again, to hear her knees creak, her knuckles
pop, the ash of her cigarette hiss and flare.

She gargled with salt water, spit it into the sink,
grabbed the phone with her claw, the back of her head

sleek as a crow. My mother is a crow on my lawn,
laughing with the others, flapping up on a branch,

jerking and twisting her ruffed neck, looking around.
I find her everywhere, her eyes staring out from aspen bark,

the rivers of her hands, the horse's ankle bones.
Astounding such delicacy could bear such terrible weight.

Ode to Gray

Mourning dove. Goose. Catbird. Butcher bird. Heron.
A child's plush stuffed rabbit. Buckets. Chains.

Silver. Slate. Steel. Thistle. Tin.
Old man. Old woman.
The new screen door.

A squadron of Mirage F-1's dogfighting
above ground fog. Sprites. Smoke.
"Snapshot gray" circa 1952.

Foxes. Rats. Nails. Wolves. River stones. Whales.
Brains. Newspapers. The backs of dead hands.

The sky over the ocean just before the clouds
let down their rain.

Rain.

The sea just before the clouds
let down their nets of rain.

Angelfish. Hooks. Hummingbird nests.
Teak wood. Seal whiskers. Silos. Railroad ties.

Mushrooms. Dray horses. Sage. Clay. Driftwood.
Crayfish in a stainless steel bowl.

The eyes of a certain girl.

Grain.

Evening

Moonlight pours down
without mercy, no matter
how many have perished
beneath the trees.

The river rolls on.

There will always be
silence, no matter
how long someone
has wept against
the side of a house,
bare forearms pressed
to the shingles.

Everything ends.
Even pain, even sorrow.

The swans drift on.

Reeds bear the weight
of their feathery heads.
Pebbles grow smaller,
smoother beneath night's
rough currents. We walk

long distances, carting
our bags, our packages.
Burdens or gifts.

We know the land
is disappearing beneath
the sea, islands swallowed
like prehistoric fish.

We know we are doomed,
done for, damned, and still
the light reaches us, falls
on our shoulders even now,

even here where the moon is
hidden from us, even though
the stars are so far away.

Some things happen only once.
A molar pulled is gone forever,
a thrown spark. The invention
of the internal combustion engine,
the rivening blade of the axe,
the first axe. First flight,
ice, light, math, birth.

        And death,
we think, happens only once,
though many of us hold to the belief
some residue transcends,
some fine filament that lingers on,
the body gone into a stream of purity,
the brain a blown fuse that leaves
a bright flash, rib of arc light,
nickel's worth of energy cast out
as seed onto the friable air, weed stem
of electricity that grows no matter
how often it's hacked back,
the 21 grams we long to trust:
the soul surrendering its host.

Who could blame us for once
taking refuge in the atom's
indestructibility. We did not
invent dust but can create
great waves that envelop cities,
sunder mountains of trees, render
vast swaths of water and earth
radioactive into eternity.

Once upon a time . . .
we begin our saddest stories.
Once bitten. Once burned.
Once in a blue moon. Once more
unto the breach. We die a while
into each other's arms and are
reborn like Lazarus, like Jesus.
Once we were warriors. Once,
eons ago, some of us turned
our backs to the fire, and some
were annihilated by love.

Augusta, Maine, 1951

Who was the man who ran the bait stand,
wiry and bluff, his cap's faded logo
a hooked fish, faint, barely there,
sitting on an upturned milk crate at a card table,
Igloo coolers filled with glass eels set like a row
of saltbox houses, red with squat white roofs,
near a roadside patch of briars, a black-domed grill
cooking up a batch of hot dogs, white-bread buns
wrapped in reused tin foil, puffs of steam
escaping from the cracked blackened folds,
some unnamable, maybe flammable, amber liquid
in a mason jar from which he sipped as the sun
blared down, blot on the blue summer sky?

This is a portrait of the father I never knew,
a snapshot taken by my mother the year
before I was born, before he left this photograph
to work with the other men filing into
the brick paper mill along the Kennebec River,
the roped backs of his hands growing paler
each day, sawdust on his shoes, duff in his lungs.
But weren't they beautiful? Those nights
on the dance floor. Her black satin skirt.
Her ankles flashing. His white cuffs rolled up,
exposing his wrists as he spun her.

Where is it written that a man must love the child
he fathers, hold her through the night and into
the shank of morning, must work to feed her,
clothe her, stuff trinkets in his pockets, hide one
in a mysterious hand held behind his back,
telling her to choose? It's anyone's guess.

I will never know the man who sat by the road
that led to the ocean, though I swam
between his hip bones, lived in that kingdom,
that great secret sea, my heart
smaller than a spark inside a tadpole
smaller than a grain of salt.

Chair

Oh the thuggish dusk, the brackish dawn, morning
cantilevered over the trees, afternoons doing nothing
again and again, like pushups. Like watching
a redwood grow: fast and slow at the same time.
Clock ticks: each minute a year in your ear.
The days are filled with such blandishments, nights
brandishing their full-blown stars, the decade's
rickety bridges, baskets of magazines open-winged
on the porch, rusted wind vanes pointing north, cows
drowsing in clumps on the hills. Will you ever come back?
Will I welcome you again into this house? There are staircases
sewn to the walls throwing bolts of deckled light.
Let's breathe that air. You could sit in a chair, right here.

Urn

I feel her swaying
under the earth, deep
in a basket of tree roots,
their frayed silk
keeping her calm,
a carpet of grass singing
Nearer my god to thee,
oak branches groaning in wind
coming up from the sea.

We take on trust the dead
are buried and gone,
the light doused for eternity,
the nevermore of their particulars
ground up, dispersed.
As a child I didn't know
where the light went
when she flipped the switch,
though I once touched
the dark bulb that burned
my fingertips, studied the coiled
element trapped inside
seething with afterglow.

Arizona

The last time I saw my mother
she was sitting on the back patio
in her nightgown, a robe
thrown over her shoulders, the elbows
gone sheer from wear.

It was three months before her death.
She was hunched above one of the last
crossword puzzles she would ever
solve, her brow furrowed
over a seven-letter word for tooth.

I was staying at a cheap hotel, the kind
where everyone stands outside
their front door to smoke, a cup
of hotel coffee balanced
on the butt end of the air conditioner,
blasting its cold fumes over
the unmade bed. The outdoor
speakers played *Take It Easy*
on a loop, and *By the Time*
I Get to Phoenix and *Get Back*.

It wasn't the best visit. My sister's house
was filled with dogs, half-grown kids
and piles of dirty clothes. No food
in the fridge so we went out
and got tacos, enchiladas and burritos
from the Filibertos a few blocks away,
a squat tub of guacamole and chips,
tumblers of horchata, orange Fanta
and Mr. Pibb, a thousand napkins.

Everyone was happy while they chewed.

The state of Arizona is a box of heat
wedged between Las Vegas and Albuquerque.
Not a good place to be poor or get sick or die.
My mother rode a train from Maine in 1953
—she was just a girl, me bundled in her arms—
all the way to California. I've tried to imagine it.

If you continue west on Route 66
it will branch upward and dump you
into the spangle of Santa Monica
where I used to live, and then you can
drive Highway One almost all the way up
the Redwood Coast to Mendocino.
I used to do that. I probably spent more time
in my car than any house I lived in.

My mother never knew where I was.
She'd call and leave a message,
"This is your mother" (as if I might not
recognize her voice), "and I'm just wondering
where you are in these United States."
She used to make me laugh. The whole family
was funny as hell, once. Dinnertime was like
a green room full of stand-up comics.
That day, sitting with them over spilled salsa,
I saw the damage booze and meth can do
to a row of faces. The jokes were tired
and the windows behind them filled
with hot white sky, plain as day.

When I got back to the hotel it was getting dark,
but it had cooled off so I took a walk around
the parking lot. Strangers leaned out over

their second-floor balconies and shouted down
at their friends traipsing away in thin
hotel towels toward the tepid blue pool.
The moon was up, struggling to unsnag itself
from the thorny crowns of the honey locusts,
the stunted curbside pines.

I left my tall mother on the couch where
she was sleeping, flat on her back, her robe
now a blanket, her rainbow-striped socks
sticking out like the bad witch beneath
the house in the *Wizard of Oz*. But she
was not a bad witch, nor was she Glinda,
that was my mother's brother's wife's name.
We called her the bad witch behind her back.

My mother still wore her wedding ring,
even after she remarried. Why spend good money
on a new one when she liked this one perfectly well.
She always touched it like a talisman,
fretted it around her bony finger.
Three kinds of braided gold: white, rose and yellow.
By the end, the only thing keeping it
from slipping off was her arthritic knuckle.
I don't know what my sister did with it
after she died. I wonder if all that gold
was melted down in a crucible, the colors
mixing, a muddy nugget.

I do know that Route 66, in addition
to being called the Will Rogers Highway
and The Main Street of America,
was also known as the Mother Road,
from John Steinbeck's *The Grapes of Wrath*.
My mother looked like a woman Walker Evans

might have photographed, with her dark
wavy hair, wide forehead and high cheekbones,
one veined hand clutching her sweater at the collar,
her face a map of every place she'd been,
every floor she scrubbed, every book she'd read,
every ungrateful child she birthed that lived or died,
every hungry upturned mouth she fed,
every beer she drank, every unslept night,
every cigarette, every song gone out of her,
every failure. Severe, you might say.
She always looked slightly haughty,
glamorous and famished.

I saw all the cars parked in that lot and wanted
to hotwire one with a good radio, drive away,
keep driving until the ocean stopped me,
then hairpin up the coast and arrive
like an orphan at Canada's front door.

If I'd known I'd never see my mother again,
I wouldn't have done much different.
I might have woken her, taken her tarnished
shoulders in my arms, rocked her like a child.
As it was, I bent over her and kissed her
on the temple, a curl of her hair caught
for a moment in the corner of my lips.
This is my mother I thought, her brain
sleeping beneath her skull, her heart
sluggish but still beating, her body
my first house, the dark horse I rode in on.

Letter to My Dead Mother

Dear White Raven, Dear Albino Crow.

Time to apologize for all the times I devised
Excuses to hang up the phone.

Dear Swarm of Summer Sun, Dear Satin Doll.

You were my panic in a dark house, my mistake,
My maybe, my heart drain, my worst curse.

Dear Scientific Fact, Dear Cake Batter Spoon.

I love you. I love you.

I knew after I fell for the third time
I should write you, Dear Mother.

Dear Pulse, Clobber, Partaker, Cobbler.
Dear Crossword, Crick, Coffeepot, Catchall.

You told me when you were 72
You still felt 25 behind your eyes.

Dear Underbelly, Bisection, Scimitar, Doge.
Dear Third Rail. Dear Bandbox. Dear Scapegrace.

How could I know—I want to go home.
Don't leave me alone—Blank as a stone.

Dear Piano.

You played for no one, your fingers touched the keys
With naked intimacy.

At the science fair we looked in a two-way mirror
And our eyes merged.

Dear Wreck. Dear Symphony.
Dear Omission. Dear Universe.
Dear Moon-in-the-sky like a toy.
Dear Reason for my being.

You were the Emergency Room Angel
In a gown of light, the injured flocked to you.
You could not heal them all. Dear Failure.

No one on earth more hated
Or loved: your warm hands,
Your cold heart.

Dear Mother, I have tried. I think I know now
What you meant when you said, I'm tired.

I have no song to sing to your Death Star.
No wish. Though I kissed your cheek
And sang for you in the kitchen

While you stirred the soup, steam
Licking our faces—crab legs and potatoes—
Those were the days.

Acknowledgments

The Ampersand Review: "Ideas of Heaven"
The BAKERY: "Evening"
BOAAT: "Arizona"
Catamaran Magazine: "Heart of Thorns"
Cortland Review: "Changeable Weather"
Gulf Coast: "Ant Farm"
Oxford American: "Chair," "Error's Refuge"
The Pedestal Magazine: "Ode to Gray"
Poetry Northwest: "Augusta, Maine, 1951"
Plume: "Lapse"
Southern Humanities Review: "Piano with Children"
Tinhouse: "Before Surgery," "Death of the Mother"
The Well Review, Ireland: "Urn"
Willow Springs: "Crow"

"Only as the Day Is Long" and "Under Stars," Academy of American Poets, Poem-A-Day
"Letter to My Dead Mother," Montreal International Poetry Prize Anthology, Vehicule Press, UK

Thank you first and always to Joe for his unwavering faith and faithful attention, to Jill for lending me her ear and support, to my daughter Tristem for her spirit, to Wilton for his encouragement, to Michelle, Michael and Nancy who see me through, to Rosen for his abiding friendship, and to my mother who made me and gave me music.

Thank you to Michael McGriff for transcribing *Awake*, and to my students who have inspired me and given me hope for the future of poetry.

Gratitude to VCCA where some of the new poems were written, NC State for sabbatical time, and my colleagues and students at Pacific University.

In memory of my teachers, Steve Kowit and Chana Bloch, and my mentor and friend, Philip Levine.

Notes

"Lapse" is a "Golden Shovel," a form Terrance Hayes invented in which one takes a line from a poem by Gwendolyn Brooks and uses each word in the line, in order, as the new poem's end words.

"Death of the Mother" uses the end rhymes from John Donne's "Holy Sonnet 7."

"Heart of Thorns" was written about folk singers Anna and Elizabeth.

"Ode to Gray" is for Sharon Olds.

Index